Profound and practical, Robin Chaddock offers wisdom, tips, and tactics on communication in all relationships. *How to Get a Smart Mouth* will help you improve your relationships with family, friends, co-workers, and others you encounter on a regular basis.

Brenda Nixon,
National parenting speaker,
author of *Right from the Start* (Revell, '09)

I strongly recommend this excellent book. The words we speak have more power than most of us may realize. Robin has used a negative expression, "smart mouth," and transformed it into an expression with a positive meaning. To have a smart mouth means that I use wisdom in choosing my words and know when to speak and when not to speak. The truths of Scripture, the power of the Holy Spirit, better communication, and commonsense are explained in this book in such an excellent way that we can all develop smart mouths!

Lane P. Jordan, national speaker, singer, author of
12 Steps to Becoming a More Organized Woman and
12 Steps to Becoming a More Organized Mom
www.LaneJordan.com

This book is not fluff. It has enough grit and real help-me-change-for-the-better advice and commonsense wisdom to make me want to read this book slowly and then read it again. Robin Chaddock's wisdom mingles with her storytelling prowess and professional training to create a tool that can most definitely change lives for the better. *How to Get a Smart Mouth* is a treasure trove for men and women of all ages, whether in a quest for self-improvement or as a basis for group discussions.

Patricia Lorenz, author of 11 books, including
Life's Too Short to Fold Your Underwear, and contributor to
Chicken Soup for the Soul books and *Daily Guideposts* devotional

How to Get a Smart Mouth

Robin Chaddock

HARVEST HOUSE PUBLISHERS
EUGENE, OREGON

Italics in Scripture indicates author's emphasis.

Cover by Garborg Design Works, Savage, Minnesota

HOW TO GET A SMART MOUTH

Published by Harvest House Publishers
Eugene, Oregon 97402
www.harvesthousepublishers.com

Chaddock, Robin.
How to get a smart mouth / Robin Chaddock.
p. cm.
ISBN-13: 978-0-7369-2123-7
ISBN-10: 0-7369-2123-0
1. Oral communication—Religious aspects—Christianity. I. Title
BV4597.53.C64C43 2007
241'.672—dc22

2007019265

Printed in the United States of America

08 09 10 11 12 13 14 15 16 / BP-SK / 10 9 8 7 6 5 4 3 2 1

Acknowledgments

This book would not be possible without the wisdom I have gained through 23 years of marriage to my remarkable husband, David. His work as a marriage and family therapist and his impeccable example of what it means to be a wise, loving, and effective interpersonal communicator have brought me great insights and inspiration.

I am happily indebted to my technical support guru, Scott Sandstrom. Through his brilliance regarding the ins and outs of technology and his constant vigilance and availability, I have the courage to communicate using a computer.

Remarkable people gave me stories and ideas for this book. Because of them, real life is breathed into the pages as they share how communicating for better or for worse has impacted them. These very special contributors are: Marilyn Bedford, Beth Campbell, Tiffany Carr, Catherine Carvey, Lenore Chernenko, Myra Cocca, Sally Conkle, Linda Crissman, Kathy Daniels, Cheri Davis, Carolyn Dorsey, Jay Geshay, Marcy Haboush, Becky Hagarty, Janet Harris, Heather Hilman, Elizabeth Hoagland, Rev. Karen Lang, Dr. Donna Lazarick, Rev. Joan Malick, Randy Riemersma, Denise Rounds, Mary Rowe, Libby Sandstrom, Brian Shivers, Dr. Mary Schwendener-Holt, Kathy Thornton, and Cheree Williams. There are also contributors who have requested their names not be used.

Lynne Ford of WBCL-FM in Fort Wayne, IN, is a trusted friend and knowledgeable advisor in the area of communication. Her belief in this work led her to interview me about the book before it was published! That interview produced healthy insights and thoughts that made this book richer and more nourishing.

Are there people in your life you should just have lunch with more often? My friend Taylor Estes, without even realizing her brilliance, over lunch one day helped me clarify that in this book we are not only talking about being good communicators, we are also talking about communicating for good. Taylor is a powerhouse example of both.

I am very grateful for my time as an adjunct faculty member at Ivy Tech Community College of Indiana where I taught Public Speaking, Interpersonal Communications, and other classes for several semesters. The course materials and very interesting and involved students helped me sharpen my thinking and practice good and wise communication.

My editor, Barbara Gordon, serves as a model to me of someone I can trust when it comes to communication. She builds a nest of friendship and care around the authors she edits. In the safety of that nest, I can trust her when she tells me that something needs work, and I can trust her when she tells me something is really good. Barbara knows how to speak the truth in love, and that engenders lasting and productive community. Through her 20 years at Harvest House she has touched countless lives, most who don't even know she exists, because she teaches the front line how to have a smart mouth.

And finally, I thank the gracious Spirit of my Loving Creator who sustains me, guides me, and makes every day an adventure.

Contents

Introduction

I had a favorite pair of jeans. I loved those jeans. They fit just right, they were extremely comfortable, and they were pretty sturdy. Those jeans were my buddy until the day I grazed a piece of metal on the garage door and a tiny hole formed at the seam just outside the knee. The fabric began to show signs of strain. Every time the jeans were washed the gap got bigger. Eventually I had a hole in the knee from one side seam to the other. Although my daughter's generation doesn't see anything wrong with this look, I finally got rid of them. The jeans weren't wearable anymore. I could have patched them, but they just never would have felt the same.

Community is like pieces of fabric. Threads are woven back and forth to make the material strong, durable, and beautiful. What happens when the fabric gets worn away in one spot or a puncture occurs that severs the threads? The fabric starts to break down, holes get bigger with stress, and the garment is eventually ruined.

We each live in all kinds of communities. A marriage is a community. So is a family. We may have a community of colleagues in a work or volunteer setting. Certainly our churches are communities, as are our neighborhoods. Sometimes we get to choose the people in our community, sometimes we don't. But we always get to choose how we treat them and what we say to and about them.

Each of us is a very powerful and influential person. Sometimes we may not feel that way because of our personality or the age or stage we find ourselves in life. Yet each of us wields enormous sway in the lives of others because we have the gift of communication. Yes, I know what our teachers and parents said to us when people teased us on the playground or we were the butt of an unkind sibling's joke. They encouraged us with the singsong, "Sticks and stones may break my bones, but words will never hurt me." But frankly I would rather be hit with a stone than stung by some of the words people have said to and about me. A bruise I can ice. A wounded spirit takes more intensive and extensive care.

As a college teacher on topics of family and relationships, I am constantly amazed by the amount of time students want to spend in the area of communication. They want to talk about conflict resolution, learn how to heal from past hurts, speak so they can be heard in their families, and develop a nondefensive stance in listening. And that's great! Communication is the foundation of all we have with each other.

So how do you get a smart mouth? And what do I mean by a smart mouth? Certainly I'm not talking about the bane of our parents' lives when they consistently said to us, "That smart mouth of yours is going to get you into trouble!" Having a "positive" smart mouth is best summed up in this quote: "Wisdom is knowing when to speak your mind and when to mind your speech." While we'll spend more time on wisdom in chapter 1, it bears mentioning here that wisdom is the foundation of good communication:

- Wisdom enables us to make good choices. Speaking wisely is nothing more than making a series of good choices as we choose our words, our responses, and our listening style.
- Wisdom signals we listen to the "third voice" in every conversation. We stay tuned to the Holy Spirit. We walk closely with God and let that closeness inform how we communicate.

- Wisdom has companions such as peace, abundant life, and pleasantness (Proverbs 3). With wisdom we experience less stress, more sleep, and a deep sense of well-being from life lived well.

Having a smart mouth facilitates these riches in your life. It means living a life of wisdom when it comes to everyday speaking and listening. There is really nothing we do more frequently than communicate. We will enhance the fabric of our relationships or punch holes and wear the material threadbare by how we exchange words. Are you weaving stronger fabric or ripping the fabric?

Most of all, having a smart mouth is based on being a person of deep, genuine, God-inspired love. God is love…ultimate love. To love one another is the new commandment Jesus gave repeatedly in the Gospel of John (13:34-35; 15:17). Love is how we're going to change the world. The book of Proverbs tells us Wisdom has been love's companion since before the beginning:

> The LORD brought me forth as the first of his works,
> before his deeds of old.
> I was appointed from eternity,
> from the beginning, before the world began.
> When there were no oceans, I was given birth,
> when there were no springs abounding with water;
> before the mountains were settled in place,
> before the hills, I was given birth,
> before he made the earth or its fields,
> or any of the dust of the world.
> I was there when he set the heavens in place,
> when he marked out the horizon on the face of the deep,
> when he established the clouds above
> and fixed securely the fountains of the deep,
> when he gave the sea its boundary
> so the waters would not overstep his command,
> and when he marked out the foundations of the earth.
> Then I was the craftsman at his side.

I was filled with delight day after day,
rejoicing always in his presence,
rejoicing in his whole world
and delighting in mankind.
Now then, my sons, listen to me;
blessed are those who keep my ways.
Listen to my instruction and be wise;
do not ignore it.
Blessed is the man who listens to me,
watching daily at my doors,
waiting at my doorway.
For whoever finds me finds life
and receives favor from the LORD.
But whoever fails to find me harms himself;
All who hate me love death (8:22-36).

When the apostle Paul started his essay on love in 1 Corinthians 13, the first element he talks about is speech. He points out that speech may be eloquent and impressive, but if it's not rooted and grounded in love, the result is empty and meaningless. Love is the core foundation of what it means to have a smart mouth.

Calling ourselves Christian doesn't automatically make us loving. Love is a verb, not a feeling. We have to decide every day to speak and act in loving ways. We also need to depend on the Spirit of God to guide us into what it means to love as we realize more and more that we are deeply loved by our Creator. To have a smart mouth requires us to grow in understanding that we need to be transformed ourselves through the gifts of God's healing, insights, and honestly living in his grace. Author Willa Cather said, "Where there is great love, there are always miracles." To have a smart mouth means we extend the miracle of those gifts to others.

When we're talking about having a smart mouth, we're not talking just about being good communicators. We're focusing on communicating for good as well. We're interested in getting our points across *and* learning to get along with others. We want to make an authentic contribution to and a difference in God's world in his name. We are interested in helping God with his hopes and dreams for his creation.

As we learn to be good communicators and to communicate for good, we become better versions of ourselves. We learn more deeply what makes us tick and what we think is important. We learn about our beliefs, attitudes, and values. We learn that we are interesting and complex persons interacting with a world full of other interesting and complex people.

As we become better communicators and communicate for good, we find that people, situations, and history are impacted by the way we communicate. We discover communication is indeed transformational when done wisely and in the healthy framework of what God hopes and dreams for his creation.

Communication is unavoidable. Even when we're silent, we're communicating. Even if we think we're invisible in our nonverbals or inaudible in our verbals, we are still communicating. So we might as well learn how to maximize our communication influence for good!

And finally, communication is irreversible. First impressions are important. Words we say to people we're close to can never be unsaid. If we don't communicate well, we leave impressions we don't want to leave. We convey messages that can never be erased. The effects of our words and our silences will be long remembered after a particular situation is over. How wonderful if we learn to communicate in ways that we don't want to reverse!

In this book we will look at the truths of Scripture, communication theory, and common sense mixed together to form some very sound ways for us to develop smart mouths. Communicating is a huge part of our lives, and if we try to tackle it all at once, we may find ourselves floundering and discouraged. But wisely taking the journey one step at a time, strengthening our lives one thread at a time, we will find great success in transforming our speech and our listening into dynamic forces for good.

The first four chapters address wisdom, honesty, self-awareness, and listening. These are the foundation on which the other chapters are built. Getting a firm handle on the first four chapters is important because we'll refer to them on a regular basis as we discuss confrontation, forgiveness, encouragement, and justice.

The middle four chapters of the book look at two very important and sometimes daunting aspects of interpersonal communication: conflict and critique. Through our exploration we'll discover that success in these two potentially touchy areas is all in the approach, vision, and hoped-for outcome.

The last five chapters focus on the beautiful community fabric that's woven with the threads of forgiveness, encouragement, decency, advocacy, and quiet.

This book doesn't provide communication Band-Aids and quick fixes. To get a smart mouth, be willing to get to know yourself and God, and to evaluate and reevaluate your goals as someone who is constructing and protecting the cloth of community.

Each chapter has a section called "Sound Checks" to help you evaluate where you are now and a section for reflection called "Morsels to Chew On" that will enable you to savor and digest the information and encouragement of each communication principle. While this can be done very well alone, you will find exploring communication through this book with a group to be a very rewarding, insightful experience. And interacting with a group gives you more practice in using your smart mouth!

Enjoy the journey as you develop your dynamic influence and strengthen loving relationships with God, yourself, and the people in your life.

1

Setting the Smart Mouth Table

A humble knowledge of oneself is a surer road to God than a deep searching of the sciences.

Thomas à Kempis

I love Isaiah.

In the Old Testament, we have a great story of his encounter with the living God. Isaiah seems to know the importance of his mouth when it comes to living the life God has called him to live:

> In the year that King Uzziah died, I saw the Lord seated on a throne, high and exalted, and the train of his robe filled the temple. Above him were seraphs, each with six wings: With two wings they covered their faces, with two they covered their feet, and with two they were flying. And they were calling to one another:
>
> "Holy, holy, holy is the Lord Almighty;
> the whole earth is full of his glory."
>
> At the sound of their voices the doorposts and thresholds shook and the temple was filled with smoke.
>
> "Woe to me!" I cried. "I am ruined! For I am a man of unclean lips, and I live among a people of unclean lips, and my eyes have seen the King, the Lord Almighty."

> Then one of the seraphs flew to me with a live coal in his hand, which he had taken with tongs from the altar. With it he touched my mouth and said, "See, this has touched your lips; your guilt is taken away and your sin atoned for."
>
> Then I heard the voice of the Lord saying, "Whom shall I send? And who will go for us?"
>
> And I said, "Here am I. Send me!"

In this exchange, Isaiah's first thought regarding his ability to be in God's presence and a servant to the people of Israel was that his mouth was a problem. And he believed the whole nation was offensive to God. In his wisdom Isaiah knew that being in proper alignment with God and being able to carry out all God wanted him to be and do would hinge on his ability to have a smart mouth, a mouth that was set to speak well and to speak for good.

The same can be said for any of us. Our ability to be used by God to impact the world for him starts with a realistic understanding of ourselves in relation to God, ourselves as humans, and an awareness of how we communicate and why. This is the foundation of wisdom in speech.

"BASIC REALITIES" SOUND CHECK

How are you doing on the basics of communication? Rate yourself on each statement using this scale:

5=ALWAYS 4=OFTEN 3=SOMETIMES 2=RARELY 1=NEVER

____ 1. I'm aware of my own beliefs, distractions, and perceptions when someone is talking to me and when I'm talking to someone.

____ 2. I'm aware that other people bring values, beliefs, and attitudes to their interactions with me. I know no one sees the world exactly as I do.

____ 3. I'm aware of the Holy Spirit's presence, influence, and help when I'm communicating with others.

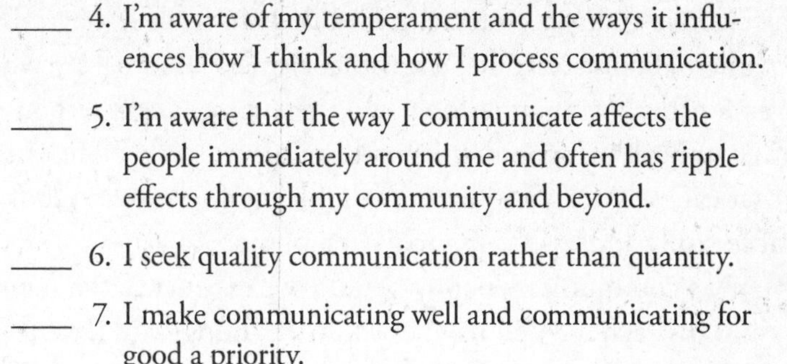

____ 4. I'm aware of my temperament and the ways it influences how I think and how I process communication.

____ 5. I'm aware that the way I communicate affects the people immediately around me and often has ripple effects through my community and beyond.

____ 6. I seek quality communication rather than quantity.

____ 7. I make communicating well and communicating for good a priority.

How did you do? If your score is in the 30 range, you understand some fundamentals of good communication, and this chapter will help you fine-tune your skills. If your score is midrange, around 20, your communication will be more effective as you apply the information in this chapter. If your score is in the lower range, you can become a better communicator. As you read through this chapter, think of specific situations that will benefit from the information you're learning.

Let's take a look at some of the basic realities we need to understand to become good, loving, transformational communicators.

Reality #1. We communicate out of our own perceptions. Our family history, faith history, set of beliefs, values, and attitudes color the way we receive information and the way we communicate. Our experiences are the lenses through which we see our world.

Being aware of our own perceptions helps us understand that our motivations and states of being are often involved in what we are able to hear, how we interpret the messages we receive from others, whether we choose to react or respond, and how we communicate our reply.

We can experience an inability to communicate. Sometimes we hear too much internal "noise." We may be mad at someone else or preoccupied with other thoughts while someone is speaking to us. A bad memory or negative emotion may be triggered by what someone has said. We may be carrying a deeper frustration or sense of guilt that blocks our ability to interact with others in healthy ways. This type of internal noise often has a spiritual element. As we'll see when we dive more deeply into this book, lying, gossiping, angry responses, and other unhealthy modes of communication are based on fears and lacks that can be spiritual in nature. Thank goodness we can look at and successfully address those as children of God.

Often we communicate poorly because we experience the "noise" of physical distraction. We may be sick, tired, hungry, or have to go to the bathroom. These can all be dealt with, some more quickly than others, to help clear the communication channels for more effective, healthy, and smart communication.

As we'll see in many of the instances of unwise communication shown in this book, having inadequate information inhibits our ability to communicate. Because of this, it's important to remember that none of us has the entire picture of truth. As Paul shared with his Corinthian friends:

> We know only a portion of the truth, and what we say about God is always incomplete. But when the Complete arrives, our incompletes will be canceled...We don't yet see things clearly. We're squinting in a fog, peering through a mist. But it won't be long before the weather clears and the sun shines bright! We'll see it all then, see it all as clearly as God sees us, knowing him directly just as he knows us! But for right now, until that completeness, we have three things to do to lead us toward that consummation: Trust steadily in God, hope unswervingly, love extravagantly. And the best of the three is love (1 Corinthians 13:9-10,12-13 MSG).

We may be able to clear up some of our missing information by listening, asking good questions, and seeking to understand another more fully. Some things we may never be able to get to the bottom of. The wisest things we can bring to our communication are openness to the understanding that we don't know everything and the overarching concern that our communication be the continuation of love.

Reality #2. Other people are working from their own perceptions. Just as each of us communicates out of our own set of perceptions, everyone around us is doing the same thing. So we need to be aware of others: where they've come from, what's happening in their lives, and what their values, beliefs, and attitudes are. This will take us a long way in helping them understand what we're saying and helping us understand what they're saying. Since we don't always know what's happening in the lives of the people around us, giving them the benefit of the doubt and listening well will enable us to communicate positively to help make God's hopes and dreams for the world come true.

Sometimes we need to communicate what we feel called to say in a situation and let God do what he needs to do with each person involved. We can't and shouldn't try to make people think a certain way. They work from their perceptions, backgrounds, and values to grow and communicate.

Several people may be involved in the exact same situation but will be processing it from very different points of view. I recently had a lovely experience in this wonderful lesson. Six of us sat quietly in white wicker rocking chairs, letting the cool southern Georgia morning air and the early morning chat of the neighboring birds waft over us. We listened to the quiet voice of our guide, "The Lord is my shepherd, I shall not want…"

As we listened to the warm and nurturing voice of our leader, she encouraged each of us to drink in the words of this very familiar poem and pay attention to the thoughts rising in each of us about how we, as individuals, were being led. She encouraged us to let our focus rest on the words that were becoming clear to us as the food the Spirit was bringing provided the nourishment we needed for our particular leg of life's journey.

This wise guide knew not to tell each of us what to think about the passage. We each needed to attend to the voice of God for our own reflections of what he was saying to us.

Realtiy #3. The Holy Spirit is always ready to be active in each of us and is always hovering around us, poised to help. Jesus said he was sending the Holy Spirit to us to be a constant force in our lives: "I will talk to the Father, and he'll provide you another Friend so that you will always have someone with you. This Friend is the Spirit of Truth...The Friend, the Holy Spirit whom the Father will send at my request, will make everything plain to you. He will remind you of all the things I have told you. I'm leaving you well and whole" (John 14:16,26-27 MSG).

Sometimes it's easy to get overwhelmed with the amount of information on being a good communicator, so it's good to know that we can rely on the promise of Proverbs 3:5-6: "Trust in the LORD with all your heart and lean not on your own understanding; in all your ways acknowledge him, and he will make your paths straight."

There's no way this book can address all the available theories, tips, and checklists to cover every situation you will face. As you read through the book, you'll occasionally think, *Yes, but you don't know...*or *But what about this type of situation?* Some situations you encounter will require you to depend on God as you discern what needs to happen in your particular circumstance.

Reality #4. We need to stay balanced in how we approach communication. All of us have preferences depending on our temperaments. Some of us work more from our heads. Some of us work more from our hearts. Some of us like to make decisions quickly and have things sewn up. Some of us like to ponder, muse, and put off decisions as long as possible. Some of us process our thoughts out loud. Some of us process our thoughts internally, preferring to think something completely through before saying anything. A keen understanding of our own preferences and the awareness that others have their own preferences will take us a long way in communicating effectively. At times we have to work outside our preferences to better connect with others. We don't ignore who we are; we just become open to new ways of thinking, processing, and communicating.

To grow as a person and as a communicator, you may be called to use your logic as often as your emotions in certain situations, even though trusting your feelings is more your style. To grow, you may be challenged to slow down and not take action until you have gathered a lot more information, or you may be challenged to take some kind of action before you comfortably have all the information you normally want.

Reality #5. We are all interconnected and our communications have ripple effects. We affect people directly, but we also touch people who are not in our direct realm. And that's not even mentioning the people in future generations our actions will impact! Our words, attitudes, and behaviors are forces for better or worse. C.S. Lewis once observed that we are each and all in the process of creating demons or angels on an everyday basis. Theologian Frederick Buechner likened our life together to a spider's web. When there is an impact on one part of the web, the entire web shakes, vibrates, and shivers. We really don't know the scope of our influence, but we can be assured that as we seek to bring love and wisdom to our everyday encounters, we are indeed making the entire world a better place.

Reality #6. Quality is better than quantity. The wry, often terse book of Ecclesiastes says, "The more the words, the less the meaning, and how does that profit anyone?" (6:11). When it comes to having a smart mouth, Scripture, theory, and common sense all point to less is more. Well chosen words go a lot further than lots and lots of words not thought out.

I still get a giggle out of thinking about the advice my otherwise gentle maternal grandmother consistently gave to my sometimes wordy maternal grandfather who happened to be a preacher. She would say, "Stand up, speak up, shut up!"

Reality #7. Communication must be a priority. Anyone who wants to build relationships with others, whether friends, family, or coworkers, must place great importance on communicating with those people.

This means setting aside time that is free from distractions, such as the phone, the Internet, and the television, for talking and listening to these important others. Several critical things happen when we do this. First, the people realize they are indeed special to us. This can have lovely transformational results in itself. Second, we have increased knowledge and understanding of the other people. Third, we give and get information that is going to be important to the smoother running of our lives.

We will watch these realities come through time and again as we walk through the chapters of this book. In the fabric of our community they are like anchor threads through which all the other threads are woven to create the tapestry.

The 7 Realities

Reality #1. We communicate out of our own perceptions.

Reality #2. Other people are working from their own perceptions.

Reality #3. The Holy Spirit is always ready to be active in each of us and is always hovering around all of us, poised to help us communicate well and for good.

Reality #4. We need to stay balanced in how we approach communication.

Reality #5. We are all interconnected, and our communication will have ripple effects.

Reality #6. Quality is better than quantity.

Reality #7. Communication must be a priority.

Understanding and applying these realities grounded in love is the foundation for having a smart mouth.

Morsels to Chew On

1. What does self-awareness mean to you? How well do you know yourself? How much emphasis do you place on your own perspective?

2. Do you allow for the perspectives of others? When has understanding others facilitated communication? When has lack of understanding made communication difficult?

3. How does the Holy Spirit impact your communication?

4. Of the temperament choices talked about in Reality #4, which best describe you? Are you balanced? If not, how could better balance improve your communication?

5. What's your take on quality of words versus quantity of words? What is your experience regarding this?

6. Who do you want to communicate with the most? What can you do to improve communication with this person?

Dear God, as I embark on this journey, please give me the wisdom to stay open to your Spirit. Help me to understand myself and others more fully so I can engage in clear, loving, and healing conversation. Help me make good communication and communicating for good a priority in my life. You've given me this remarkable gift of communication, and I thank you for the confidence you have in me to use it well.

In Christ's name, amen.

We are the wire, God is the current. Our only power is to let the current pass through us.

Carlo Carretto

2

Threads of Honesty

Always be honest.
It will gratify some and astonish others.

Mark Twain

You know what I hated when I was a little girl? I hated when my mom would look at me and say, "I know you're lying. I can see it in your eyes." How did she do that? And how come that particular kind of communication always seemed to be betrayed by my eyes? I never heard anyone say anything about what else my eyes said. My eyes just always seemed to tell the truth when my mouth didn't.

I wonder if it's because honesty and integrity are fundamental to our lives together on this planet. My husband, who has been a marriage and family therapist for more than 20 years, says that when trust leaves a relationship, that relationship is in danger. He says, "Once trust has been broken, while we may still care about the other person, we start to emotionally distance and protect ourselves from them." The intimacy that keeps a relationship strong starts to erode. Trust is very hard to recapture once it has been breeched.

Establishing and maintaining trust are not the only good reasons to tell the truth. Honesty ranks first place in virtues according to the number of biblical proverbs given to its attention. People who are truthful clear the air (Proverbs 12:17 MSG), bring enduring fidelity to all situations (12:19), save lives (14:25), are a delight to those in charge (16:13; 22:11), stimulate affection and pleasure (24:26), and bring loving correction and clarity to behavior and situations (27:6).

Apparently Jesus thought telling the truth was important. He starts speaking with the phrase, "I tell you the truth" at least 26 times in the gospel of John alone!

Honesty comes right after Wisdom in establishing the foundation for what it means to have a smart mouth. When Ephesians 4:25 declares, "Therefore each of you must put off falsehood and speak truthfully to his neighbor, for we are all members of one body," we are reminded that truth is something we *are* not just something we *say.* Good character is key to good communication. We also see the affirmation that honesty's end result is a good, strong community.

Honesty in communication comes in several different forms. In this chapter we'll explore truth telling, making and keeping promises, consistency in verbal and nonverbal communication, and establishing and maintaining credibility.

Be the Truth, Tell the Truth

As I was writing this book I asked dozens of people why they thought people lie. One answer was supplied over and over: We lie to protect. We lie to ourselves to protect us from threats to our sense of self. We lie to others to protect our identity and image with them. We lie to others to protect them from something we think they can't handle. We lie about money, weight, fidelity, emotions, appearance, the past, and the future. CareerBuilder.com reports that 57 percent of job applicants lie on a resume. Lies range from "white lies" to grand webs of illusion constructed because we believe there is no other way out of a desperate situation.

All of us have been caught in lies, and all of us have been hurt by the lies of others, whether they were told to us or about us. Lies are indeed a destroyer of community in the highest degree.

Fortunately, the root of this community destroyer is spiritual. I say "fortunately" because it can be addressed by a clearer understanding of who we are in God's creation...and through a clearer understanding of God.

As we'll explore in chapter 3, we can tell the truth to ourselves because there is nothing God can't heal, redeem, or help us get through. When we tell the truth to ourselves, it's easier to tell the truth to others about ourselves and how we perceive the world. We can also tell others the truth about us because we are ultimately not assessed by their opinion of us. We are judged by God. The truth can and will set us free, even if we have to work through some significant issues to fully experience that freedom.

Why is telling the truth so important? When we tell the truth and are the truth, we set in motion the wheels that can free others from self-deception and deceiving those around them. A lighthearted yet poignant example of this comes from one of my favorite fairy tales by Hans Christian Andersen, *The Emperor's New Clothes*.

In this story we meet a royal clotheshorse who is so vain that all he thinks about is the next outfit he's going to wear in front of his subjects. He is visited by two very slick con men who have spotted his weakness and plan to capitalize on it. They offer their assistance in suiting his royal highness in threads that are so magnificent only the wise and savvy can see them. They work for weeks, all the while inviting in the king's advisors to check on the progress. Not wanting to be genuine and tell the truth (and be labeled a fool), each advisor plunges the situation into deeper darkness by fussing over the nonexistent outfit.

At last the day comes for the king to walk in front of his subjects. The word has gone out that only the "in" crowd will be able to see the clothing. Everyone gets the memo except one little guy who can't yet read. As the king is regally strutting through the streets, this genuine boy blurts out rather loudly, "But he hasn't got anything on!" Well, lightning doesn't strike the little guy, and gradually the truth sets people free. A snicker ripples through the crowd, and then some outright guffaws. Soon people are doubled over with laughter. As if the scene were not bizarre enough, the last paragraph of the story says, "This made the emperor anxious for he knew they were right.

But the emperor thought, 'I must keep up appearances through the procession.' And the emperor walked on still more majestically, and his aides walked behind him and carried his imaginary train, which didn't exist at all."[1]

Truth telling sets us free because eventually lies are heavy burdens. When we're released from those burdens, we are able to move through life without guarding ourselves or others. Henry David Thoreau said, "Between whom there is a hearty truth, there is love." There is love because nothing in all the world feels so good as being completely ourselves and feeling 100 percent accepted. When we speak the truth in love, as Paul encourages us to do, he says the result is to enlighten and enliven people to be who they were meant to be and to carry on the work they were meant to carry on (Ephesians 4:15).

This leads us to an important and deeper dynamic. *Being* the truth and *telling* the truth enables others to be and tell the truth themselves. There are times in our closest relationships, the ones that are ongoing and need to be tended with long-term care, that we know someone else is not being or telling the truth when they are interacting with us. These are tricky situations, requiring great love, compassion, skill, and awareness of what the other person may be trying to protect in not being honest. The purpose of confronting a lie is not to embarrass the person or to put ourselves in a position of judge. Instead, it's to clear the air, to make the relationship more transparent and intimate, to help him or her see that protection isn't necessary. Ultimately we tell the truth about ourselves and help others tell the truth about themselves to set all of us free.

People who are by design more intuitive will sometimes say, "I just know something isn't right here." They can tell by nonverbals and tone of voice. What are the clues to spotting a lie? Paul Ekman specializes in social interaction cues. He has found that deception can be detected in three ways. Ekman calls them "leaks."

- *Voice.* The voice of a person not telling the truth may tremble or break, especially if they are feeling strong emotion about their lie. Rate of speech can be another clue. A person who is speaking faster than normal may be angry, slower than normal, sad.

- *Body language.* Common body language "leaks" are sudden swallowing and rapid breathing, which may indicate nervousness.
- *Facial expressions.* These seem to be the most noticeable "leaks," the ones we usually cite when we can tell someone is lying. A phony smile, eye shifts, trembling lips, and even facial tics can clue us. Because there are forty-three distinct facial muscles that create facial expressions, they are more difficult to mask and control than body movements or tone of voice.[2]

Mercy, tact, and understanding are the best tools for dismantling lies. Tact is the social grace of helping someone "save face." When we confront people with their lies, our main goal is redemption and liberation. People will often be embarrassed and defensive about lying, but if they are surrounded by the tools just mentioned, the issue can be dealt with gently and the community restored and nurtured.

"Honesty" Sound Check

Honesty is the glue that holds relationships and communities together. We need to be able to be honest with ourselves and with others to build and maintain the trust we need to grow stronger. Respond to each statement using this scale:

5=ALWAYS 4=OFTEN 3=SOMETIMES 2=RARELY 1=NEVER

____ 1. I know my potential to lie so others will think I'm something I'm not or that I'm not something I am.

____ 2. I embrace the reality that there is nothing about myself that God can't heal, redeem, or help me get through.

____ 3. I use tactful honesty, compassion, and love in helping others look at the truth about themselves…even when it's tricky.

____ 4. I keep the promises I make.

____ 5. My nonverbal communication matches my verbal communication so others won't be confused by my communication.

____ 6. I strive to be credible with others, even if I have to say things they may not want to hear.

The scale for this Sound Check is 6 to 30. If your score is close to 30, you are very honest with yourself and others. You tell the truth to yourself about yourself, are seen as someone others can count on, and have strong credibility in your relationships. If you have a lower score, are there one or two areas in particular that give you trouble? Spend some time with the ideas in this chapter to see which ones will help you lay a better foundation for honest communication.

Promise Making and Keeping

The second way we tell the truth and have a smart mouth is in keeping our promises and expecting others to do the same. As Stephen Carter said, "Promises are the bricks of life and trust is the mortar."

Keeping our promises honors the power of covenant that is key to our understanding God. Throughout the Old Testament, Yahweh made promises with key people. Faithfulness was the foundation of these covenant pacts. The history of faith is based on God being true to these commitments. Our understanding of God in history lays the foundation of our relationship with God today.

In the New Testament, Jesus said his life and work on our behalf was the new covenant of love and redemption God wanted to establish with his creation. Jesus' promise was to be the redemptive bridge from God to us, to show us more fully the nature and intention of God toward us, and to keep the communication lines between our Creator and us open, loving, and alive. We become Christians because we count on God in the flesh and God in Spirit to be true to us, to never lie to us. Promise making and promise keeping are the foundations of our ongoing relationship of hope and grace with our Creator.

When it comes to us humans, though, we don't like to think breaking our promises is actually lying. It was merely an oversight, it slipped our minds, we just couldn't get to it. But Proverbs 12:22 has a word for those who can't, don't, or won't keep promises. Eugene Peterson sums it up graphically in *The Message:* "God can't stomach liars; he loves the company of those who keep their word" (Proverbs 12:22).

Faithfulness in our speech is evidenced when we say what we mean and we mean what we say. My friend Karen told me the difference a promise kept can make in a person's life. She and her son went grocery shopping one evening. Part of that night's bounty were goodies for a sack lunch the next day. Michael was excited, looking forward to taking special treats with him to school.

The next morning Karen's household, which included a very busy husband and three kids, was bedlam. Homework was flying into backpacks, hair was hastily brushed, cereal and milk were flowing at a rapid rate. There was simply no time to pack the much-anticipated expression of a mother's love—the special lunch.

Michael went to the bus a very sad little boy. Big tears flowed as he explained how much he'd looked forward to his lunch full of the good things that had been so carefully chosen the night before.

Karen has a deep love for her children, but she also had a physical therapy appointment and a lunch scheduled that morning. But the more she thought about it, the more she was convinced she needed to keep her promise to her son. She packed his lunch box and drove nearly 30 minutes to deliver the precious, promised lunch. She related later to me at lunch that she would never forget the look on her son's face when she walked into the room and handed him his lunch. Not only did Michael become more convinced of his mother's love for him, he subconsciously reaffirmed that God is faithful and can be trusted.

It's not news to any of us that good communication takes time and concentration. That's one of the reasons it's hard to keep our promises at times. We run out of time to complete a promised task. We're so overloaded we forget to follow through on what we've said we'll do. We sometimes secretly hope the other person will forget what we promised and we'll be off the hook. Fortunately or unfortunately, my kids have ironclad memories for things I have promised I will do or buy for them. Honesty, once again, becomes a spiritual issue. And we need to examine how we are living our lives: Has anything become more important than keeping our promises?

And promises don't always start with the words, "I promise..." Simply telling someone we will do something is a commitment to action. "I'll call you later." "Let's get together for lunch next week." "I'll have that proposal to you in the morning." Speaking words that indicate we're going to do something means we need to follow through to maintain trust, community, and faithfulness.

Now there are indeed times when we can't keep our promises. We sometimes speak too soon or overstate our abilities or intentions. These situations call for stark humility and honesty. Proverbs 6:1-5 offers last-resort advice when you've promised something you can't or won't deliver:

> Dear friend, if you've gone into hock with your neighbor or
> locked yourself into a deal with a stranger,
> If you've impulsively promised the shirt off your back and now
> find yourself shivering out in the cold,
> Friend, don't waste a minute, get yourself out of that mess.
> You're in that man's clutches! Go, put on a long face;
> act desperate.
> Don't procrastinate—there's no time to lose.
> Run like a deer from the hunter, fly like a bird from the
> trapper! (MSG).

Breaking a promise should be a last resort. In those cases, we still must be honest with the person we're dealing with.

Verbals and Nonverbals Need to Match

Communication is not only about what is spoken. We communicate nonverbally all the time. Studies even show that more of us believe the nonverbal messages a person sends than the verbal messages we may believe we are receiving. For example, if I meet you at the door and say, "I'm so glad you're here," but I'm not smiling, I keep my hands in my pockets, and I stay planted in the door frame, chances are excellent you're not going to believe I'm really glad you're here. Every day across the nation a child spills or breaks something. While Mom may say, "It's okay," the child knows from her tone of voice that it's not. Dad may say, "Don't worry about it," but the look on his face produces plenty of worry. Grandma or Grandpa may try to reassure, but their postures may say otherwise. Kids believe the nonverbals and wonder why adults don't tell the truth!

We can serve as wonderful family members, friends, and colleagues when we are observant of and verbal about other people's nonverbals. We can often tell more about what people are experiencing by how they look than by what they say. Watching for cues from the eyes, mouth, hands, and posture gives us plenty of information.

So we need to keep track of our nonverbals and make sure they reflect that we're truthful and credible. We make a large impact by the countless ways we communicate without saying a word. Make sure that result is positive!

Credibility

When we tell the truth to the best of our ability (as we perceive it in particular situations), we become more credible, trustworthy, and believable to people around us. This seems to be particularly true when speaking truth that potentially puts us at odds with others or when it might not be the savvy or popular stance. Catherine tells of a time her truth telling established her credibility for a long-range relationship, even though the first encounter was tricky.

> I was the executive director of a nonprofit that worked with various federal agencies. Most of the members of the

> nonprofits were people from small, rural communities. Diversity meant there was more than one church.
>
> As I sat down at a meeting early in my career as executive director, one of the staff from the Indiana office of this federal agency asked me why I thought he had so much trouble with some of the members. I responded, "You're black."
>
> As you can imagine, he was a little taken aback, as were several other members of his staff. But I went on to explain that the majority of the members had not grown up with blacks and had definitely not had a black person in a position of authority over them. I, on the other hand, had gone to an inner-city high school and had had people in my life who were close to me who were black.
>
> Although this could have had a long-ranging negative effect, he seemed to appreciate my candor, and it set the tone for the next eight years we worked together.

Establishing and maintaining credibility is an act of faith. When we are willing to communicate in this honest way, we indicate we are willing to speak the truth as we see it and let others respond or react the way they need to. We are willing to trust that our truthfulness is pleasing to God, even if others don't respond positively. We open ourselves to the "Micaiah Syndrome." In 1 Kings 22, we find Jehoshaphat, king of Judah, and Ahab, king of Israel, contemplating an act of war. Should they or shouldn't they? All of Ahab's prophets tell them to go ahead and do it. The prophets are convinced they will have victory. Jehoshaphat is not so convinced:

> But Jehoshaphat dragged his heels: "Is there still another prophet of GOD around here we can consult?"
>
> The king of Israel told Jehoshaphat, "As a matter of fact, there is still one such man. But I hate him. He never preaches anything good to me, only doom, doom, doom—Micaiah son of Imlah" (verses 7-8 MSG).

> The messenger who went to get Micaiah said, "The prophets have all said Yes to the king. Make it unanimous—vote Yes!"

But Micaiah said, "As surely as God lives, what God says, I'll say."

With Micaiah before him, the king asked him, "So Micaiah—do we attack Ramoth Gilead, or do we hold back?"

"Go ahead," he said. "An easy victory. God's gift to the king."

"Not so fast," said the king. "How many times have I made you promise under oath to tell me the truth and nothing but the truth?"

"All right," said Micaiah, "since you insist.

> I saw all of Israel scattered over the hills,
> sheep with no shepherd.
> Then God spoke: 'These poor people
> have no one to tell them what to do.
> Let them go home and do the
> best they can for themselves.'"

Then the king of Israel turned to Jehoshaphat, "See! What did I tell you? He never has a good word for me from God, only doom."

Micaiah kept on: "I'm not done yet; listen to God's word:

> I saw God enthroned,
> and all the angel armies of heaven
> Standing at attention
> ranged on his right and his left.
> And God said, 'How can we seduce Ahab
> into attacking Ramoth Gilead?'
> Some said this,
> and some said that.
> Then a bold angel stepped out,
> stood before God, and said,
> 'I'll seduce him.'
> 'And how will you do it?' said God.
> 'Easy,' said the angel,
> 'I'll get all the prophets to lie.'

> 'That should do it,' said God.
> 'On your way—seduce him!'
>
> "And that's what has happened. God filled the mouths of your puppet prophets with seductive lies. God has pronounced your doom."
>
> Just then Zedekiah son of Kenaanah came up and punched Micaiah in the nose, saying, "Since when did the Spirit of God leave me and take up with you?" (verses 13-24 MSG).

Apparently Zedekiah was one of the seduced prophets.

Micaiah had the opportunity to be a "yes man." He chose instead to act on God's truth, to maintain his credibility even when it cost him a bloody nose.

Most of us are not prophets of Israel, and we have more common encounters that test our credibility. I deeply appreciate the witness of one of my friends who shows a gracious and honest way to maintain credibility. She balances care for the other person with adherence to her belief in telling and being the truth:

> I recently read in the newspaper of a woman I know who is being indicted for fraud. She is a passive co-owner of a business that made profits in a fraudulent way. I couldn't believe my eyes when I read the article. I don't know her well, but I remember our past associations as pleasant and kind. Anyway, she called me on Sunday, asking me to be a character reference for her. Talk about difficult! I suspect she was just too passive in her ownership and let the other owner basically run amuck with the business, but, nonetheless, she is responsible. She has young children and is now facing prison time if she is convicted.
>
> I don't know her well at all. I've just had a few opportunities here and there for a quick, "Hi, nice to see you again." How do I not help her, yet how *can* I help her? I hardly know her. She is desperate; she needs someone who will tell the judge she is not a lawbreaker. Her voice and her words were pleading with me to help. As she explained how everything

> had happened, I prayed very quickly that God would lead my words as I responded. I finally told her that it had been years since we had last seen each other, let alone talked, but that I had always thought she was a great mom and a very nice person, and I would be happy to testify to that. I would not be able to say much more, but I could do that much. She calmed down and was so grateful for even that little bit. I cautioned her that it probably wasn't what she needed for her court case, but it would be another character reference she could have in her file.
>
> This may not seem like much, but I had never been faced with this situation before and haven't a clue what she was asking me to get myself into. If I hadn't caught the article in the paper, I would have been clueless. It was as if I were primed for this phone call, and God saw me the rest of the way through. I've yet to receive the court paperwork, so we'll see where this goes, but I'm calm about my involvement.

My friend promised to tell the truth. She knows the limits of her knowledge in the situation. While we're often tempted to appear to know more than we do or we're enticed to overstep the boundaries of our appropriate involvement, establishing and maintaining credibility mandates that we keep a wise watch over our words.

Morsels to Chew On

1. Why is trust so important to the foundation of relationships?

2. We lie in two ways: with our mouths and with our lives. Think back to one of your most memorable verbal lies. What were you trying to protect? Now recall one of your most memorable life lies. What were you trying to protect?

3. What spiritual truth did you need to be clearer about to not commit the lies in question 2? Do you now have a better understanding of God?

4. What significance do Jesus' words, "You will know the truth, and the truth will set you free" have for you? (See John 8:32.)

5. Without being specific about names or details (if you're in a group), have you ever been lied to or about? How did you handle the situation? What did you like about how you handled it? What would you change?

6. Reflect on a time when a promise was made to you and kept. What did you experience? Reflect on a time when a promise was made to you and not kept. What did you experience?

7. What are some of the challenges to promise keeping?

8. When has your credibility been tested? How did you handle it? What was the outcome?

Loving God, thank you for always being truthful with me. Your truth does indeed set me free. Thank you for your promises and for keeping every one. I can relax with you in trust and openness.

Forgive me for the times I don't tell the truth or live the truth. Help me become so deeply aware of your love that I don't need to wrap myself in verbal or life lies to protect me or anyone else.

By your Holy Spirit, enable me to live a life of truth. Strengthen my ties with you and with others.

In Christ's name, amen.

Being entirely honest with oneself is a good exercise.

SIGMUND FREUD

3

Don't Let Your Mind Eat Junk Food

Nothing is a greater impediment to being on good terms with others than being ill at ease with yourself.

Honoré de Balzac

"You're worthless."

"Why are you even trying? You've never done it right before, why do you think you can now?"

"For heaven's sake, just give up this quest. You'll never improve."

"Stop fooling yourself and everyone else. You're just a loser."

"You don't deserve it."

Imagine someone feeding you a steady diet of this junk food thinking. Hopefully you would feel a little bit of anger and resentment toward that person. How dare he or she talk to you like that!

Yet many of us aren't at all upset with feeding ourselves the same steady diet. We completely undermine our ability to be good communicators who communicate for good because we don't communicate positively with the source of a wise, smart, and loving mouth—ourselves. Communication experts call it intrapersonal communication, and it is, quite literally, the foundation for interpersonal communication. You can't weave beautiful, sturdy cloth with damaged, frayed, weak, and rotting threads.

In our time together exploring how to get a smart mouth, we'll look at how we confront others, how we tell the truth to others, how we forgive, speak decently to, offer critique to, and encourage others. But none of that will have any authenticity if we don't first know how to do it internally. The way we talk to ourselves has gigantic ramifications for the way we talk to others. And the internal state of our hearts and minds affects the quality of our communication. "What comes out of the mouth gets its start in the heart" (Matthew 15:18 MSG). At the core of what Jesus stated to be the second most important commandment is that we love ourselves before we can love anyone else (Mark 12:31). So how well do you talk to yourself? How healthy, nourishing, and uplifting is your self-talk?

"JUNK FOOD" SOUND CHECK

Because good communication starts with good self-talk, we need to be sure our hearts and minds are speaking in a healthy, loving way to ourselves. Respond to each statement using this scale:

5=ALWAYS 4=OFTEN 3=SOMETIMES 2=RARELY 1=NEVER

____ 1. I understand that my communication with others will only be as healthy as my communication with myself.

____ 2. I believe that as a beloved child of God, I have the opportunity to have my mind and heart continually renewed by God's Spirit.

____ 3. I tell myself the truth about me, including the positives, negatives, mistakes, lacks, and hurts I have in my life.

____ 4. I'm willing to constructively confront myself when something that needs changed or healed comes to my attention.

____ 5. I forgive myself for what I do that I don't want to do and for what I don't do that I want to do.

____ 6. I give myself good, positive, realistic critiques so I will grow strong and confident and improve in my communication.

____ 7. I see myself as God sees me.

____ 8. When needed, I encourage myself with a little pep talk and review my positive attributes.

____ 9. I keep my heart and mind open to the "sighing" of God within me that helps me better understand what he wants for me and what he's created me for.

The scale for this Sound Check is 9 to 45. The higher your score, the healthier and more positive your self-talk. If your score is in the 40s, you maintain a steady flow of positive conversation with yourself about yourself. You can look at the things you need to change without fear or self-abuse, and you celebrate the things that make you a unique child of God. The higher your score, the more positively you influence your environment as well.

Where Transformation Begins

Where does transformation of the world begin? In your mind. In the renewed mind the seeds of the good and perfect hopes and dreams from God are planted and cultivated. Paul's letter to the Romans spells this out with delicious clarity: "Do not conform any longer to the pattern of this world, but be transformed by the renewing of your mind. Then you will be able to test and approve what God's will is—his good, pleasing and perfect will" (Romans 12:2). Eugene Peterson translates this verse to read, "Don't become so well-adjusted to your culture that you fit into it without even thinking. Instead, fix your attention on God. You'll be changed from the inside out. Readily recognize what he wants from you, and quickly respond to it. Unlike the culture around you, always dragging you down to its level of immaturity, God brings the best out of you, develops well-formed maturity in you" (MSG).

Communities and cultures that aren't aware of or respectful of or blatantly disregard God's ways are marked by deception, hurtful confrontations with no redemptive intent, unforgiveness and grudge-holding, mean-spirited backbiting, and discouragement. As people renewed and always renewing by our relationship with God, we're encouraged by Paul to put this kind of treatment out of our heads—literally out of our minds and we're not to talk to ourselves in these terms. When we cease to treat ourselves poorly, we'll treat others better and build relationships more aligned with God's good and pleasing and perfect will.

What are some of the marks of this kind of mind transformation?

Self-Honesty

There are no other lies quite like what we tell ourselves about ourselves, our pasts, the people who have impacted us, our current conditions, and our futures. We usually lie to ourselves to protect ourselves from the anxiety that would be caused if we told the truth. In fact, if we look at the root of most of our anxieties, we'll find a lie. It's often a lie about who we are in God's world and in God's heart. Someone else may have directly told us a lie about who we are, we may lie about ourselves to protect others, we may have picked up the lie just from being around someone else, or we may have picked up a lie through the belief system of a whole community. Lots of lies start in childhood, so they're tough to name, much less confront.

Many of the lies we tell ourselves have to do with our pasts, the relationships we didn't understand when we were children, and mistakes we made that we just as soon nobody know about. To face the truth would expose lacks, hurts, and bad choices, and that can seem too much to handle. Yet in very deep and profound ways, these are exactly the things that were nailed to the cross on Good Friday and completely redeemed on Easter by the death and resurrection of Jesus.

My friend Donna said, "Denial is also a way of lying to ourselves to keep from knowing the truth, which can be tough or hurt. For example, I have been able to lie about the impact of my weight gain after my mom passed away. I have recently been confronting the layers of that lie."

Donna is a wise and brave woman who is also a psychologist and life coach. She's allowing me to share her story of what she describes as the layers of self-lies she's confronting even now. Several years ago, she experienced the deaths of two women who were very close to her. Because her life was a whirlwind of two children, a traveling husband, her own career, and what she calls "unfinished business," Donna was exhausted and depressed. She found delicious comfort in sweets. The weight she gained and the health she lost helped her keep her mother close by becoming like her.

Donna's mother had a stroke history and congestive heart failure from diabetes. When she died suddenly of a virus, Donna had not gotten to say goodbye to her. Her last conversation with her mom was about her mom's desire to visit and see Donna's ten-day-old son, Daniel.

Not only did the sweets shape Donna's body into a body much like her mother's, they also contributed to a diagnosis of Type 2 diabetes.

Further adding to her self-deception and denial, Donna's doctor became terminally ill as all of this was transpiring, so she avoided his office.

Through some soul-searching in meditation and prayer, and with a supportive group of friends surrounding her, Donna began to face and address the lies that were festering in her life—lies about love, worthiness, beauty, and keeping the ones we love in memory.

Over time and through layers, Donna decided she can honor her mother in ways that aren't self-abusive. She chose to believe the truth she's had planted deeply inside that her friends have been drawing out of her: She really can and needs to love herself. She opted to open herself to positive and bountiful supplies of love living around her in the forms of her husband, children, friends, and associates. She decided to redefine beauty. She believes God is truly moving her forward in her endeavor to take good care of herself. She is open to the idea that nourishment can come in ways other than sweets and comfort food.

Self-Confrontation

Confrontation for the sake of confrontation is like backing into a 12-inch bank of snow with your car and expecting to get out easily. You'll go nowhere. The only good reason, the only godly reason, to have a confrontation with anyone, ourselves included, is to bring something to light that needs changing and then make a plan to change it.

As a life coach, I'm a very big fan of setting intentions, making choices, and getting clarity on where you are now and where you want to be. But these can only be authentic and effective forces when we've done the deeper work of taking responsibility to be fully and actively in partnership with God to heal the wounds that need healing, forgive the predisposition to go our own way, clear away the debris of lies told to us and about us, and make peace with people for hurts (real and imagined). In *12 "Christian" Beliefs That Will Drive You Crazy,* Drs. Henry Cloud and John Townsend tell the story of a woman who continually vows to change her behavior, only to find that she winds up back in the same hurtful and limiting patterns she's always lived because she didn't know to go to the deeper level of self-confrontation and the deeper acceptance that comes from this type of childlike honesty before a loving Creator.

Self-confrontation is not blasting away at ourselves for being who we don't want to be and not being who we think we should be. Self-confrontation is a *loving* look at thoughts, beliefs, and behaviors that are not making us the best version of ourselves. We need to discard those and build into our lives the thoughts, beliefs, and behaviors that make us more Christlike.

We can't just make a vow to get a smart mouth and set out to work really hard to make it happen. We partner with God's Holy Spirit to gently excavate what needs to be changed and set about truly being transformed by the renewing of our hearts, souls, minds, and strengths.

Self-Forgiveness

Without going into all the details on forgiveness that you'll find in chapter 10, let's touch on self-forgiveness. The principles and processes of forgiveness are particularly potent when applied to ourselves.

Not forgiving ourselves cripples our ability to communicate well and for good. When our spirits and heads are cluttered with the noise of rattling chains and creaking doors of living in the haunted house of self-destructive self-anger and hatred, our perceptions of ourselves and of the intentions and motives of others bear the cobwebs of muddled and suspicious interactions. We never quite know what's going to pop out and scare the life out of us.

Maybe we can't forgive ourselves for not being like a favored sibling. We don't forgive ourselves for intentionally hurting a colleague. We don't forgive ourselves for taking that drink that led to the abuse of a beloved spouse or child. We don't forgive ourselves for walking out of a marriage even though it included a life-threatening situation. We don't forgive ourselves for something nobody else even knows about. Whatever we don't forgive in ourselves, we have a hard time trusting God to forgive in us.

Yet the reality is that to clear the path for health, life, and vitality to flow into us and out to others, forgive ourselves we must. Communities are not built in hostage-holding situations.

If you want to read more on this, go ahead and skip to chapter 10.

Self-Critique

My friend and mentor Mary Rowe worked as a career counselor for a good part of her career. Her observation of students was that good, positive, realistic self-talk is essential to someone being able to successfully pursue jobs they want. When we critique ourselves in a solely negative way, we inhibit our ability to land in positions where our gifts and skills can be used. Ultimately, as Christians, that can mean we're not partnering with God to bring about his hopes and dreams for his creation. So how can we start viewing ourselves more positively? A good beginning is a resume. Mary Rowe shares:

> An exercise to build good self-talk is writing a resume. The entire job search process requires it. Often from my position

> as a college job placement person, I saw poor self-talk inhibit students. One of the little joys was guiding them to discover how to find and talk about their strengths. I kept a 3x5 card under my desk blotter with some leading questions on it. If we got "stuck," I would slip the card out and use the questions to help move the experience along. Such things as:
>
> - What is your best quality as a worker?
> - What do you like best about yourself?
> - Why should someone hire you?
>
> Whatever the student answered I would immediately write down. Together we explored that idea, massaging the words until they fit.

Even if we're not seeking a job, we can write a life resume that highlights our God-given talents, skills, passions, and interests. These come quite literally from God, and we can celebrate with him the beautiful creation of us by recognizing and using our gifts in a spirit of gleeful gratitude. Think of yourself realistically from *God's loving point of view.*

Okay. Think about this scene to its logical and spiritual conclusion. I'm at a retreat designed to help people discover their "divine assignments." As part of the excavation process, I encourage each person to write a poem about themselves in the same fashion that Proverbs 31 is written (regarding the woman of virtue). When Hebrew writers wanted to write a poem about something, they put the letters of the Hebrew alphabet down the side of a paper, and then wrote out the characteristics of their subject based on the particular letter of the alphabet.

So in this exercise, I encourage the participants to write 26 positive characteristics describing themselves. Invariably someone balks, saying they can't think of anything good to say about themselves. For some deeply wounded people, this may be true, and they will need more loving attention than can be found in a weekend group retreat. But some people have been *trained* to not think well of themselves and that this is a virtue. This *is not* humility. The logical and spiritual conclusion is they aren't honoring God, their Creator. They aren't stepping out of their "humility" long enough to see themselves as God's partner, gifted to be and do what God needs them to be and do. And that's not helpful to self, community, or God. Nothing is going to be transformed with this mind-set.

Now, there most certainly will be moments when we discover something that needs work. So isolate one item at a time, being very specific about what you want to address. "I'm such a failure" is going to be much less helpful to you than "I would like to have more success as a (parent/student/banker/neighbor)." Take two or three emotional steps back from the flaw and ask yourself how it got there. Then brainstorm several options for addressing the flaw. Choose one and get started! Make sure to draw yourself a mental or word picture of how you and the community will benefit from the correction of this flaw.

Self-Encouragement

One Christmas I fell in love with a neat little book I received as a gift. It was called *When God Asks…A Chance to Change* by Richard Wilkins. The premise of the book is a small question on each of the 147 pages that begins, "When God asks…" and ends with "…what will you say?"

An interesting little question that corresponds with this idea of self-critique is, "Do you encourage more than you criticize?" At first blush, we may think this question is asking how we treat others. And that is a good question. But when it comes to building greater self-awareness and enhancing our abilities as communicators, this question can be applied to how we talk to ourselves too.

When we are critical of ourselves, when we put ourselves down, we're not being humble. In fact, it usually leads to us being obsessed with ourselves as we constantly compare ourselves to others and wonder what they think of us.

When we encourage ourselves, we allow ourselves to appreciate who we are as creatures made by our loving Creator. Then we can relax, stop obsessing about ourselves, and get on with the wondrous work God has given us to be about.

Positive, realistic self-talk gives us the strength to "feel the fear and do it anyway." Positive, realistic self-talk won't wipe out fear. In fact, where there is no fear, there is no courage, because there isn't any need. Dorothy Bernard observes, "Courage is fear that has said its prayers."

God planted you on this earth in just the place you are geographically at just the right time in history for his purposes. To reach maximum capacity to be a good communicator who also communicates for good, your heart and mind need to be as clear as possible of negative self-assessments, anger, resentment, and faulty notions of yourself, God, and others. Why? Because the Spirit of God is living in you and is trying to communicate!

Who Gets to See God?

Recently while sitting in Sunday worship service, I heard a familiar passage in an unfamiliar way. The preacher talked about the Spirit of God in each of us communicating with our Creator in a way that is far too deep for words. Some Scripture versions translate this "sighing" (Romans 8:26-27 MSG). The sighing is the heartbeat of what God is calling each of us to, and it's as diverse in each of us as we are from each other. I'd never thought of it like that before.

Has your spirit ever sighed in you? Have you felt something stirring in your heart that you couldn't quite put words to? Maybe it's a piece of the greater vision God has for his creation that he's given for you to carry but you lost it in the negativity, unresolved relationship, unaddressed hurt, or unexplored wonder.

We clear our hearts and minds for the sighing to have a more perfect connection with God when we are honest, gently confrontational, forgiving, respectfully self-critiquing, and encouraging of ourselves. We will do a much better job of offering these vital community-builders to others if we offer them to ourselves first.

Jesus pronounced who would get to see God in his Sermon on the

Mount: "Blessed are the pure in heart, for they will see God" (Matthew 5:8). Why is this so? Because those who are pure in heart have nothing standing between them and their Creator. There's wonderful, open communication. Miss Alice in Catherine Marshall's book *Christy* makes this observation, "The only time I ever find my dealing with God less than clear-cut is when I'm not being honest with Him. The fuzziness is always on my side, not His."[1]

One of my goals is to keep things clear between God and me. My intention is to keep a pure heart, although I may not always have a perfect heart. I want to do this because Jesus said if I do, I will be able to more clearly and authentically connect with God. And this connection can't help but enhance the communication I have with others as I see myself more clearly—my attitudes and perceptions, my prejudices and points of vulnerability. I'm not saying I'll always have everything "cleaned up" before I talk to God. Instead I'll take the whole crazy mess to him no matter what so we can sort everything out together.

Clarity of heart and thought makes for a very smart mouth. Stay clear by staying honest, loving, and wise with yourself.

Morsels to Chew On

1. Why is self-communication so important for becoming better, wiser, and more loving communicators?

2. "Don't become so well-adjusted to your culture that you fit into it without even thinking. Instead, fix your attention on God. You'll be changed from the inside out. Readily recognize what he wants from you, and quickly respond to it. Unlike the culture around you, always dragging you down to its level of immaturity, God brings the best out of you, develops well-formed maturity in you"

(Romans 12:2 MSG). As you reflect on this passage, what comes up for you?

3. Knowing there's nothing you have to face about yourself, your past, or your future that can't be healed, redeemed, or loved by God, where do you need to be more honest with yourself?

4. What do you need to forgive yourself for? What have you left undone that needs forgiveness?

5. Create an alphabet poem as described in the Self-Critique section. Put the alphabet down the left side of a paper and write one of your positive character traits, gifts, skills, talents, or interests for each letter.

6. Identify a personal flaw you want to tackle. Be specific, be compassionate yet a little emotionally aloof, and decide two or three things you can do to correct the flaw.

7. Where do you need some encouragement right now? Jump ahead to chapter 9 if you need some ideas for encouraging self-talk.

8. "Friends, I'd say you'll do best by filling your minds and meditating on things true, noble, reputable, authentic, compelling, gracious—the best, not the worst; the beautiful, not the ugly;

things to praise, not things to curse" (Philippians 4:8 MSG). How does applying this change how you think about yourself? About your relationship with God?

9. How is the Holy Spirit sighing within you? Is there something new you need to explore?

Gracious God, thank you that I can be healthy in mind and positive in thought because of the transforming work of your Holy Spirit working in me to reveal your hopes and dreams for me and for your world. Thank you for specific ideas you've given me to make my thoughts about myself healthier, more nurturing, and more aligned with what you intended when you created me.

Forgive me for the times I treat myself poorly by talking unkindly and untruthfully to myself. Help me realize that the way I think of and talk to myself sets the stage for how I view and treat others.

Renew me by transforming my mind by your grace.

In Christ's name, amen.

Friendship with oneself is all-important, because without it one cannot be friends with anyone else.

ELEANOR ROOSEVELT

4

Listen Up!

The most called-upon prerequisite of
a friend is an accessible ear.

Maya Angelou

This chapter is evenly tied with the first three for importance in laying a solid foundation of being a good communicator who communicates for good. Listening well is fundamental to true communication.

When we think of communicating well, we often think about saying things in a way that gets our point across. But true communication is a complete cycle of exchanging information, ideas, and feelings. We haven't truly communicated until we've also listened...and listened well.

Listening is essential for conflict resolution and for growing in intimacy with God and others. Listening brings encouragement to people in ways that speaking simply can't convey. So having a smart mouth means having smart ears too.

Listening well has some basic principles.

1. *Listening is not the same as hearing.* We can't help but hear if our auditory organs and nerve transmitters are working properly. Hearing is the process of receiving

sound waves and having them encoded in the brain. Hearing is the first part of listening, although people who can't hear can still listen, as odd as that sounds. Listening is intentional. We focus on what we're hearing. It's done with the ears and also with the mind, the heart, and the eyes. Listening is a choice.

2. *Listening is an active process.* We decide not to daydream while another person is talking. We decide that the other person's message requires our care and interaction. Listening means we decide that building a relationship with the other person is more important than other activities at this point. Listening is a singular activity; it's not very well done when our attention is divided.
3. *Listening is a skill that can be learned.* It requires that we understand our own perceptions and possible tendencies to be ineffective listeners. Listening well grows as we mature in love and wisdom.

Why Is It Hard to Listen?

There are at least six reasons why it's hard to listen:

1. *The speaker is boring.* Everyone knows what it feels like to be involved with someone who won't stop talking or who speaks so slowly we wonder if he or she is ever going to finish. Our eyes glaze over. We start making mental grocery lists. We feel the urge to yawn. We want to get away as soon as possible.
2. *We're thinking about our own opinion and what we're going to say when it's our turn.* This kind of listening is self-centered.
3. *We feel overwhelmed by what the person is saying* because the content is too complicated, technical, or

out of our areas of expertise. This type of listening is not meant to be disrespectful; we tune the person out because he is essentially talking in a language we don't readily speak or understand.

4. *We feel smothered by content that is too emotionally loaded.*
5. *We assume the other person is going to be wrong, and we're waiting to catch him in his "wrongness."* This is "judgmental listening." We're not really interested in what the other person has to say. We want to catch him in a lie, an inconsistency, or with erroneous information.
6. *We have some kind of "noise" going on ourselves.* We may have internal physical distraction like pain or thirst. We may have an external physical distraction like music playing too loudly in the next room. We may have internal psychological or emotional noise, such as being angry with someone (not necessarily related to the person speaking).

None of these conditions assist in strengthening the threads of community. One of the most dangerous effects of not listening well is that we end up with incomplete information. Consider what could happen if the following scene was in the wrong sequence.

A good friend called to talk to my husband one day. Our friend lived out of town but called David to tell him he was here for a funeral. Our friend's mother had died.

David was writing down bits and pieces of the conversation, getting a detail or two here and there. Fortunately David had the chance to tell me the whole story before I found a note on the counter that said, "(Our friend's name), died, service Friday, (phone number)." I would have freaked out!

Not listening fully to what someone says is very much like reading that incomplete note. We may misunderstand, miss critical pieces of information, and jump to way off-base conclusions.

Now, let's look at some basic ways to become better listeners.

❧ "LISTENING" SOUND CHECK ❧

We have two ears and one mouth for a reason. Respond to each statement using the following scale:

5=ALWAYS 4=OFTEN 3=SOMETIMES 2=RARELY 1=NEVER

____ 1. I'm aware of the times when I'm not listening well, and I can pinpoint why I'm having trouble paying attention to the speaker.

____ 2. I ask good questions and stay engaged with what the speaker is telling me.

____ 3. I let people finish what they're saying before I respond.

____ 4. I don't assume I know what the other person is going to say.

____ 5. I reflect back to the speaker what I'm hearing to keep communication clear and eliminate misunderstandings.

____ 6. I listen with my eyes as well as with my ears.

____ 7. I know listening is not passive. Good listening is interacting with another person while he or she is talking. Listening is a powerful skill.

If your score is closer to 7, you might want to watch your listening patterns for a week or so to see where you're particularly vulnerable to not listening well. Once you have an idea of the relationships and situations that challenge your listening skills, put the information in this chapter to good use to become a better listener. If your score is closer to 35, you probably have people talking to you all the time because they love the way you listen to them!

Employ Curiosity

One way to become a better listener is to help people open up by being genuinely interested in what they're talking about. I really like Myra's description of what it means to be truly interested in someone else:

> Being genuinely interested in someone's conversation is all about concentration. I find that when I am not thinking about yesterday's happenings or my next appointment, I can really enjoy any conversation—become immersed in it—and, as a result, ask good questions and engage in meaningful dialog. It's all about being concentrated, being in the moment.

Myra points out the importance of asking good questions. Good questions are not only those that are good in content, but they are asked with genuine curiosity at the right time.

As a life coach, I've learned quite a few good, standard questions. But good questions also emerge when we're genuinely curious. They pop up. I may say to someone, "I just had something bubble up. May I ask you a question?" I am very respectful of my client's right to refuse to hear my question. But more often than not, the rapport I've established leads my client to trust me to ask good questions.

So I ask the question, and my client knows I'm truly interested and that I care. (Check out appendix A for a list of great questions that show people you're interested in them.)

Employ a level of childlike curiosity about the people you talk with. What makes them tick? What are they interested in? Where have they been, and what has influenced them? This isn't psychoanalysis 101, just a basic, wide-eyed wonder about how other human beings work. Carolyn illustrates a simple question she and her husband use to let others know they genuinely care:

> My husband and I were in our mid-twenties and had been married for over a year when it suddenly hit us that we were conversationally self-centered. It seemed like oftentimes when we got together with friends, we would leave

hearing our voices ringing in our ears with talk of ourselves. It wasn't that we weren't interested in what others had to say; it simply hadn't occurred to us to ask *them* how *they* were doing. They would ask us how we were, and we were off and running. We made a pact that we would start asking others about their lives—hopefully before they asked us. From good friends to the person cutting our hair, we always make sure we ask what's going on with them. Not only is this more polite, but it feels good to focus on others instead of ourselves.

Hear Before Speaking

Proverbs 18:13 reveals excellent insight: "He who answers before listening—that is his folly and his shame." That might come under the category of "Well, duh!" but most of us have interrupted someone, which tells people, essentially, that what they have to say isn't really all that important. Why does this happen on a regular basis? It takes time to listen to other people's ideas. It takes time to let people give input. It takes time to allow others to finish their sentences. And time seems to be in such short supply for most of us.

This is especially true with kids. A youngster begins with, "I have a great idea!" For reasons that we'll look at in more depth, a parent or grandparent will say, "No!" When that happened in my house when my daughter was young, she would stamp her foot and say, "Mommy, you didn't even listen to what I was going to say." And most of the time she was right. And when I got my head into the current situation and listened to what she had to say, sometimes it was a really great idea that led to something fun, the expediting of a task, or a special moment together.

The second reason we speak before we listen is we're feeling so provoked by what the other person is saying we want to tell him what's what right away. We'll look at this scenario more fully in chapter 6 when we talk about conflict and maturity. For now, let's heed the words of Proverbs 15:28: "The heart of the righteous weighs its answers, but the mouth of the wicked gushes evil."

A third reason we speak before we think is that we believe we know what the other person is going to say. This assumption is folly to the highest degree, as anyone will tell you who has ever done this and found out what the other person was going to say was quite different than what was anticipated. Don't assume you know what another person is going to say. This is called "mind reading," and most of us aren't very good at it.

A benefit to resisting assuming we know what the other person is going to say is that we may, if we are truly listening, hear something we've never considered.

> When a minister reads out of the Bible, I am sure that at least nine times out of ten the people who are listening will not hear what is really being read but only what they expect to hear read. And I think that what most people expect to hear read from the Bible is an edifying story, an uplifting thought, a moral lesson—something elevating, obvious, and boring. So that is exactly what very often they do hear. But that is too bad because if they'd really listen—and maybe you have to forget that it is the Bible being read and a minister who is reading it—there is no telling what you might hear.[1]

The best way to listen before you speak is to be sure the other person has finished completely. Listen first. One reason we interrupt has, at its root, a good intention. We sometimes interrupt because we're giving feedback to the other person indicating that we understand. While well-intentioned, this kind of interruption is a disruption and your conversation partner may consider it an intrusion. Don't break in until someone has completely finished his point.

Feedback, Please

Repeating what we've heard is a great way to ensure we're listening. And sometimes the other person hasn't always said what we believe we heard! Consider this tasty illustration.

> In our church we have our Sunday morning services and we have one Sunday evening service. The morning services

> are more formal and are followed with doughnuts, punch, and coffee in our community room. The evening service is more casual and is followed by chips, cookies, pizzas, and cold drinks.
>
> One day a little boy approached the woman who coordinates the Sunday school teachers and said, "I get it now! On Sunday night we have pizza, and on Sunday mornings we don't. That's why we say, 'The pizza crust be with you' on Sunday mornings!"

Whatever logic was at play for this young one, he was reflecting on what we actually say Sunday morning, which is "The peace of Christ be with you."

We often hear based on our own experiences and perspectives. Reflecting back to our conversation partner what we believe we've heard keeps communication clear and avoids misunderstandings. This is often referred to as "active listening."

The Eyes Have It

It's nearly impossible to teach about listening without mentioning the importance of eye contact. My friend Brian sums it up well: "Good listening is done as much with the eyes as it is with the ears. My father taught me this by example. I remember him holding on to my face and looking into my eyes and saying, 'Listen to me.' In return I have found myself doing the same thing with my daughter today."

Literally and figuratively, eyes are symbols of illumination and understanding throughout Scripture. Imagine Jesus was talking about the importance of listening when he said, "Your eyes are windows into your body. If you open your eyes wide in wonder and belief, your body fills up with light. If you live squinty-eyed in greed and distrust, your body is a dank cellar. If you pull the blinds on your windows, what a dark life you will have!" (Matthew 6:22-23 MSG).

Jesus also highlighted the intertwined power of eyes and ears when he spoke candidly to some listeners, paraphrasing the words of Isaiah:

Your ears are open but you don't hear a thing.
Your eyes are awake but you don't see a thing.
The people are blockheads!
They stick their fingers in their ears
    so they won't have to listen.
They screw their eyes shut
    so they won't have to look,
        so they won't have to deal with me face-to-face
    and let me heal them (Matthew 13:14-15 MSG).

Apparently we need to use our eyes and our ears if we want to be fully aware and benefit from the message we're hearing.

Far More Than Just Being Quiet

While listening can appear to be a passive activity, it truly changes people...and so it impacts the world. It enables greater clarity, deeper faith, stronger self-understanding, and increased love for others. Sally reflects on the benefit of having someone in her life who truly listens:

> I wonder how many hours I have spent driving down the road and letting the same thoughts chase each other in my mind. I wonder how many nights I have gone to bed with those same thoughts running around aimlessly, waking me at two o'clock in the morning. I wake at two with "the answer" and fall back into a restless sleep, only to realize with the sound of the alarm that the same thoughts are back. I have a vague remembrance of solving this problem during the night, but as the day begins I find myself right back where I started. I know I am not alone in this behavior. I get emails from friends sent in the wee hours of the morning. I watch colleagues stumble in some days weary from a night of tossing and turning.
>
> The thoughts tend to chase themselves when left alone, but I have found there is a way to corral them, to herd them in and make them work for me. There is a huge value in finding someone who is a good listener. These people are few and far between, and if you have someone like that in your life, you should consider them a treasure. They have the rare

> ability to be quiet, to sit in silence, to ask the perfectly timed question or raise a point that allows your mind to get back on track and stop running rampant. These are the people in your life who are honest, who do not judge, who bring out the real you.
>
> Allowing that person into your life often seems risky. It seems easier and safer to keep things to yourself, to allow those thoughts to run down the old familiar trails. We are sometimes afraid of what we might find if we allow ourselves to be exposed or vulnerable to another person. I have found, however, that allowing another to come into my life, to ask me the hard questions, to make me stop, breathe, and look within, is the surest way to find the answer I have been looking for. It is the quickest route to finding the answers I have been seeking. The real answers always seem to come from within, but it takes a guide to take us to the deeper parts of ourselves where we can mine the gold.

Truly listening is a much deeper exercise than just being quiet while someone else is talking. Being a good listener means we are interacting with another person while he or she is talking. When we listen well, we listen with our hearts and our minds, our ears and our eyes. And is there anything so wonderful as the feeling we get when we know someone "got it" when they were listening to us? We can spread that feeling by listening to others, by showing they matter and are truly important to the fabric of our community. We show them they have a wondrous place in God's world!

Morsels to Chew On

1. Reflect on a time when someone listened to you with his or her whole heart. What was it like?

2. How can you improve the listening situation when a speaker is boring?

3. Are you prone to interrupting? How do your conversations usually go?

4. How might you approach a situation in which the speaker's vocabulary or topic is simply not the "language" you speak?

5. When have you experienced being emotionally overloaded by the content of another person's words? How did that impact your ability to listen? How might you approach this kind of conversation to maximize the communication between you and the other person?

6. What are some options when you experience internal or external "noise"?

7. How can curiosity help us be better communicators? Have you experienced this?

8. What are some reasons you have a hard time listening before you speak? Who is this most likely to happen with in your life? How can the relationship be improved with more thorough listening?

9. In addition to good eye contact, what are some other ways you know someone is truly listening to you? What are some of your favorite ways to let other people know you are really listening to them?

Listening God, thank you for the big clue about how you want me to interact with others. You gave me two ears and one mouth. Forgive me for the times when I'm not a very good listener. I don't always listen to you, to my best self, or to others. I miss a lot of wonderful interaction because of that. I miss opportunities to make the world a better place.

Help me stay emotionally, mentally, physically, and spiritually clear so I can truly listen to others. I want to listen with a discerning, curious, and helpful spirit.

In Christ's name, amen.

There is nothing we like to see so much as the gleam of pleasure in a person's eye when he feels that we have sympathized with him, understood him, interested ourself in his welfare. At these moments something fine and spiritual passes between two friends. These moments are moments worth living.

Don Marquis

5

Straight Shooters Hit More Bull's-eyes

Making the simple complicated is commonplace; making the complicated simple, awesomely simple, that's creativity.

Charles Mingus

Less is more. This is the grueling lesson I had to learn at a workshop designed to help writers meet the media. At this workshop we learned how to pitch an idea so we can get booked on television and radio shows. What I learned is boiling a 60,000-word book into short, sound-bite sentences is excruciating for a writer. But the condensing concept certainly got me to thinking.

How much better would we be at communicating with ourselves and the people around us if we got to the point more quickly on a regular basis? Not being terse and impolite, but making our point or request clear without muddying everything with lots of explanations, apologies, and excuses. My mom shared with me a phrase she learned while becoming a marriage and family therapist: "Don't complain, don't explain." In other words, say what needs to be said and get on with building the relationship. I can tell you one thing right now... books would be a lot skinnier! My editor also has taught me a great deal in this regard. She has basically told me (this is a paraphrase), "Stop trying to look so clever—just get to the point!" I love her.

Clarity and brevity remind me of a story told about legendary theologian Karl Barth. While lecturing one day Barth was asked by a member of his audience, "Dr. Barth, what is the most profound theological truth you've ever discovered?" Barth, without much hesitation, said, "Jesus loves me, this I know, for the Bible tells me so." That's clarity and brevity!

To have a smart mouth requires three areas of willingness in communication: 1) say who you are and what you need, 2) be willing to ask, and 3) let your yes be yes and your no be no.

The Truth About You

I encourage you to be honest about what you will and won't do or be in a relationship or in a situation. Be specific and clear so people know what you are about. Many relational misunderstandings could be cleared up more quickly if we have the courage to be forthright. It's not always easy or comfortable. But people are usually a lot more flexible if they know where we're coming from.

Being clear means we get to the point quickly to cut down on confusion and misunderstanding. Don't tell people what you don't want. Imagine going into a restaurant and telling the waiter all the things you don't want from the menu. Your order will be significantly delayed. Cheryl shared a story about the power of being clear about who she was and how she wanted to see the holidays go in the wake of the nearly back-to-back deaths of her parents.

> I think I had emailed you that my dad died in September, Robin. Then my mom died on Dec. 7. So it was a tough time and a really different Christmas for my husband, son, and me. Most of Tom's family had gone on a cruise the week before the holiday, so our traditional time spent with them went by the wayside. This allowed me to grieve as I needed, to reminisce, and to just keep it simple. I didn't shop for gifts this year other than to get ornaments of fishing Santas and snowmen to commemorate my dad, which I did before my mom passed. I attached tiny headshots of my dad and tags inscribed "Gone Fishin'" above his name and dates of his life, and sent one to each of my closest family members.

The weekend after my mom died I spent long hours talking long-distance with each of my four siblings and writing "A Eulogy for Our Mom," which DeeDee, the youngest of us, read during the funeral since I chose not to go. (I'd been to North Dakota for a visit and spent truly meaningful time with Mom 12 days before she died.)

I was pleasantly surprised at how our 13-year-old son handled this downsized holiday. With dread I'd think of the stereotypical greedy teen (like I was, sad to say). Usually Niko's got at least a dozen gifts under the tree from us alone. This year there were a few small treats from other family members and some gift cards. On Christmas Eve (of all days), we spontaneously took a drive down to Brown County after church to browse the few shops that were open. During that day we discovered that Niko had an unusual dream—to ride a unicycle. We encouraged him to research how and where to buy such a thing and find guidance on riding it, which he did on the Internet during our quiet, just-us-three Christmas Day. And the next day he and his dad went out and bought a unicycle. In three day's time Niko just about mastered free-mounting, riding long distances, and turning! This may turn out to be our best Christmas yet.

I took lots and lots of time to journal and ponder the meaning of the season: God's bounty free to us, our messages about Santa, giving/receiving, the circle of life, memories. I followed my heart and communicated my wishes. My family went along with it. I didn't want this to be one of those times when I did what society dictates or what I thought other people wanted me to do. We didn't put our tree up until Christmas Eve and Christmas Day and then used a scant assortment of ornaments—my fishing Santa, of course, and paper stars that Niko had folded. I rang bells for the Salvation Army, donated blood, and gave toys to kids less fortunate. All of these things were healing for me. They were the kinds of things I felt God and my parents would be proud to know I was doing. And now I have a blessed, fresh perspective for my journey into the new year.

Contrast Cheryl's experience with a gentleman I met who wanted to research hiring me as a life coach. As we talked, getting to know each other to see if we were a good coaching match, I realized he would benefit from coaching after he got clearer with his family about what was happening.

He had, for various reasons, put his career and social life on hold for an extensive time while he was helping with larger health and parental care issues in his family. Over the course of several years, he'd done what he felt was his duty. Now he wanted his siblings to take some of the responsibility he had been shouldering. But he wouldn't tell them that he wanted this. He wouldn't speak up and let his brothers and sisters know what he thought they needed to be doing. He expected them to read his mind and take care of him and his parents. At over 50 years of age, he was way behind in career and relational development. He had become so increasingly angry with his family for not paying attention to his life that he was not in any position to get "unstuck" until he was ready to communicate clearly about who he was, what he wanted in this family relationship web, and what he intended to be and do in the upcoming months.

Samuel Butler said, "If people would dare to speak to one another unreservedly, there would be a good deal less sorrow in the world a hundred years hence." I see this dynamic oftentimes when I am under a deadline. It seems like the week before a deadline lots of requests and potentially interesting things come up. While I sometimes feel a catch of neurotic hesitation when I keep myself focused on what I need to accomplish, being clear about who I am and what I need to do with my time helps other people understand (and hopefully respect) what I'm doing and why. This also protects me from feeling resentful about being interrupted.

This kind of clarity employs what is described as a "self-defining, non-anxious, presence" by Edwin Friedman in his book *Generation to Generation: Family Process in Church and Synagogue.* Freidman suggests that all three of these qualities can be very helpful in building relationships while maintaining healthy boundaries. When we self-define, we describe and outline our life goals and values. Next comes the interesting part. Oftentimes we are able to self-define but the anxiety that produces when we perceive others may not be pleased causes us to want to get away. So true community building and honest communication come from being able to self-define and manage our anxiety to the extent that we don't feel the overwhelming urge to flee when others disapprove or pressure us to conform back into what they want for us (which is often what's least anxiety producing for them).[1]

Parenting specialists continually remind us of the importance of consistency and clarity in our communication with children. While kids may not appreciate our limits, structures, and standards at times, we enable them to experience safety and connection to us when all is said and done.

Asking Well

As you define yourself and what you have to offer the world, you'll most certainly have to ask for what you want and need from God and others. Why would Jesus say, "Ask and it will be given to you; seek and you will find; knock and the door will be opened to you. For everyone who asks receives; he who seeks finds; and to him who knocks, the door will be opened" (Matthew 7:7-8) unless he meant it?

God's hopes and dreams for the world include wholeness for each person and for all communities. When we take Jesus' invitation seriously, we evaluate:

- What we really want.
- Why we don't ask.

Honestly working with both of these questions will give us strong, beautiful, and lasting threads with which to weave our community and build wise communication. If we spent concentrated time on these two notions, we would be changed in fundamental ways. Yet we are people who are more interested in thinking up all the reasons this couldn't possibly be true rather than believing God on his terms. Maybe that's the key! We're not all that familiar with God's true terms.

So why don't we ask from God, from ourselves, from others? The payoff is clear and compelling: "Until now you have not asked for anything in my name. Ask and you will receive, and your joy will be complete" (John 16:24). What healthy person doesn't want complete joy?

Two guys, whom I call "the Chicken Soup guys" because of their prolific series of Chicken Soup books, have written a book called *The Aladdin Factor* that explores the ins and outs of the art of asking. Jack Canfield and Mark Victor Hansen cite five main reasons why we don't ask for what we need, let alone what we want.

First, many of us don't really know what's possible in our lives. We may have blinders on simply because we've never known anything outside our little family, our little town, our little state, our little country. We don't know what's available.

We may also be young, inexperienced, or out of touch with ourselves so we don't know what we want. My daughter and I recently had an interesting conversation about men, dating, and how high school girls are treated in relationships. She gave me a list of all the things that were not satisfactory about the boys she "dated" in the past, so I asked her, "Madison, what do you want?" She had a hard time telling me. I had to ask several times before we started peeling away the layers of what she doesn't want so we could get to the heart of what she does want.

Some of us don't know what the options are to effectively ask for what we need. Little children instinctively know this is important because they use all kinds of methods to get the adults' attention to let them know what they need. Unfortunately, we mostly teach them interactions of whining, indirect requests, nagging, hints, and complaining. Many of us didn't have good instruction or role models of how to ask for what we want and need in a direct, effective manner.

Second, Canfield and Hansen point out that we don't ask for what we want because of limiting and inaccurate beliefs. I have been struck by the number of times Jesus began an earthly conversation with someone using one version or another of the question, "What do you want?" I have been equally struck by the number of times I don't enter into this conversation—for it truly needs to be a conversation—with God for a number of reasons. Do any of these resonate with you?

- If I ask and don't get it, God doesn't love me.
- If I ask and don't get it, I'll be mad at God.
- If I ask and don't get it, I'll feel rejected.
- If I ask and don't get it, I must not be doing it "right."
- If I ask and don't get it, I'll look foolish, especially if I've told other people what I've asked for.
- If I ask and don't get it, I'll be miserable because I won't have what I want.
- If I ask and don't get what I want, something is wrong with God or something is wrong with me.

These responses indicate a "toxic cookie" must be present in our thinking. In my book *12 Great Choices Smart Moms Make,* I introduce the concept of the toxic cookie. Toxic cookies are little morsels we usually ingested when we were children that represent worldviews, opinions, rules, and guilt trips we "should" believe and obey. Toxic cookies are usually childish thoughts that haven't been examined in the light of new, more mature, reasoned thoughts and experiences. These cookies lurk in our backgrounds, not wanting to be discovered but definitely not wanting to be ignored.

Toxic cookies keep us from entering into a bold, free, and expectant relationship with God—the same God who was Jesus on earth who asked on a regular basis, "What do you want?"

The true key for us in asking anything of God (or of others) is to realize that this is an ongoing dialog, not an opportunity for us to lay down a list of demands. This conversation is continually refined as God keeps communicating and we keep asking and the answers unfold.

Toxic cookies are misinformation. For many of us that misinformation was about the nature and character of God. If we grew up thinking God keeps things from us to develop our character and make us "better people," it might be time for a more intimate, give-and-take relationship with God. If we grew up thinking all we have to do is ask and believe hard enough and everything we ask for will come true carte blanche, it might be time for a greater understanding that God would rather give us himself than give us stuff.

Third, a close cousin of inaccurate beliefs is the barrier of fear. In fact, inaccurate beliefs are often the cause of fear. We don't have because we don't ask because we are afraid. We're afraid we will be rejected, that we won't be taken seriously (signaling that we're not important to the person we're asking). We fear we'll be humiliated or look stupid if the person says no. We fear punishment. We may even have a deep fear that if someone complies with our request we'll be forever indebted to them.

Fourth, we don't ask because we suffer from low self-esteem, the belief "I'm not really worth it." I don't know about you, but I get increasingly irritated with people who say, "I don't want to make you go to any trouble" or "Anything you do is fine." When I've taken the time to specifically ask, I want to hear specific replies. If someone in my house doesn't respond definitively with an answer when I ask what he or she wants as a gift for an upcoming occasion, he or she doesn't get anything. Costly mistakes can be made when we try to force others to read our minds because we don't voice our preferences, needs, and desires.

Finally, Canfield and Hansen point out that a big hindrance to effective asking is good old-fashioned pride—except there's really nothing good about it. We most certainly live in a culture that salutes self-sufficiency. And being able to do things for ourselves and not be dependent on others is a sign of maturity. We try to instill this trait in our children so we're still not fixing chicken noodle soup for them when they're 25. But, as with many good things about human interactions, our culture may have taken independence to an extreme by interpreting our asking for what we need and desire as a character flaw. (Just ask anyone who has been lost but won't ask for directions.)

A crucial point in asking anything of God or of others is understanding your relationship.

> Don't bargain with God. Be direct. Ask for what you need. This isn't a cat-and-mouse, hide-and-seek game we're in. If your child asks for bread, do you trick him with sawdust? If he asks for fish, do you scare him with a live snake on his plate? As bad as you are, you wouldn't think of such a thing. You're at least decent to your own children. So don't you think the God who conceived you in love will be even better? (Matthew 7:7-11 MSG).

Sadly, national statistics bear the truth that there are plenty of parents who aren't as good as the ones mentioned in this passage. But that doesn't mean God is that way. That doesn't mean that other people are that way. We do have to have a lot of trust in others and confidence in ourselves to ask for what we need and prefer. And those qualities sometimes must be developed or repaired as we overcome hurts and hurtful relationships from the past.

We need to be bold, ask, and then step out. We will be better able to trust God's power and intentions the more we get to know him. We will be better able to ask for things of others when we trust who we are in the world and are ready to dialog with them no matter what they say.

So how does clarity in asking for what we want enhance our relationships? When my daughter, Maddie, was 15 years old, she had a lot of things on her mind. One thing that kept surfacing was getting a car. While there was no way her dad and I were going to get her a new car when the time came for her to drive, the fact she asked made the subject stick out more in our thinking. We were made aware that we needed to talk about various options that would lead to her having wheels.

That's the power of asking. When you ask for something, you make known to others what you want, need, and dream about. When you ask, you set conversations in motion that could result in attaining what you're seeking. While Maddie knows there's no earthly way she's going to have a new car given to her, had she not raised the question—had she not asked—the conversation wouldn't be happening at all. Voice your requests out loud so others around you are clear about what you seek and desire.

Janet Harris, president and CEO of Mission Coffee and Tea, is one of the most direct people I know. When I asked how she learned to ask for what she wants, she responded:

> I believe this has been an acquired skill that has blossomed after many years as a career salesperson. After college I found my "zone" in sales. The beauty of sales is that your successes (and confidence) build upon each other. I would close one sale and be fired up to knock out the next one. Part of classic Sales 101 is to "ask for the order." I guess I got this lesson and ran with it.
>
> A number of years later, I co-chaired a nonprofit's large fund-raising program that featured multiple events. (Incidentally, I was nearly nine months pregnant during most of these events, which I had not anticipated when I agreed to co-chair!)
>
> I felt a tremendous responsibility to ensure our efforts produced *big* money results. I was thus forced to ask for many donations, corporate contributions, volunteer support, and more. In my desire to avoid failure and humiliation I learned this: It is amazing what you get if you only *ask!* I mean this in the small things *and* in the large, God-sized sense. I have held to this simple philosophy with truly amazing results. Try it! Just ask…

How you ask has a great deal to do with what you receive. For example, my children can request a glass of milk in two different ways. For a gentle, sincere request I would walk to the ends of the earth and milk an insane cow for them. For a loud, demanding request I generally suggest they get the milk from the refrigerator and pour their own glass of milk.

A cute commercial highlights the beauty of children communicating—and the corners adults paint themselves into by not being direct.

A little boy and his mom are pondering the floor in their home. The mother says, "I wonder how I'm going to tell your dad that I want a new floor." The child raises his voice to yell into the rest of the house, "Dad, Mom wants a new floor!"

In many cases it's just not that hard to tell people what we want...if we'll stop over-thinking the situation. We may not get exactly what we want, but we'll never know until we try. And once we put voice to our wants and get them, we may not really want them after all. But that's a great learning experience about discovering what we really desire. It's ultimately true that we may get exactly what we need and want.

Frank Scully asks, "Why not go out on a limb? Isn't that where the fruit is?" James, a New Testament writer, gives us a framework for expressions of want to help us know which limbs to climb out on for the best kind of fruit. He says we are more likely to get what we ask when we are aligned with the Giver of all good gifts. When we are in partnership with our Creator, it's more likely we'll see the fruit because our desires match his.

So make an honest assessment of what you want and why you want it. Then get out there and ask for it! Don't make a little kid do your work for you.

Yes Be Yes, and No Be No

My clever friend and fellow Harvest House author Mary Byers lays out the most compelling reason why we should "simply let your 'Yes be Yes,' and your 'No be No'" (Matthew 5:37) in her book *How to Say No and Live to Tell About It.* Her reason strengthens the threads of community in two ways. First, it helps us be clear on who we are and what we're about. Second, if we take this reason to heart and live it with gusto every day, God's hopes and dreams will be lived through us on a regular basis.

Mary recommends that each of us find our "burning yes!" What is this? Until we have a clear understanding of what we're called to be and do, we'll mush around in life trying on all kinds of things, saying yes when we should say no, and vice versa. The clarity of our "burning yes!" or what I call our "Divine Assignment," enables us to filter and prioritize all the requests for our resources (time, money, talent, strength, mind). The ones that fit our call get a "yes," the ones that don't fit get a "no." Discovering our Divine Assignment is one of the best gifts to us, to God who gave us the Divine Assignment, and to the world who is waiting for us to live it fully. (For more information on discovering your Divine Assignment, please visit my website: www.RobinChaddock.com.)

Mary and I agree there are lots of reasons we say the opposite of what we should say to requests for our resources. Have you heard these run through your head or come out your mouth?

- "I'll feel guilty if I say no."
- "Who will they get to do it if I don't?"
- "They won't like me anymore if I don't do this."
- "My family will look like slugs if we don't say yes."

Basically we get yes and no confused because we're anxious about what others might say if we give an answer they don't want to hear. The beauty about letting your yes be yes and your no be no is that it signals you are in touch with yourself and with your Creator.

This communication clarifier keeps relationships more open, honest, and God-centered. As we learn to simply say yes or no without a bunch of other words, a great deal of pressure is taken off us. During the free-time break on Saturday afternoon while leading a women's retreat in Wisconsin, a small group of ladies went shopping. To commemorate this topic that we had discussed in the morning session, they bought me a wonderful ceramic plaque. It simply says: "Attention! 'No' is a complete answer." And may I add, so is yes when it's given for the right reasons.

"STRAIGHT SHOOTER" SOUND CHECK

Direct and clear communication makes relationships more honest and smooth. Respond to each statement using the following scale:

5=ALWAYS 4=OFTEN 3=SOMETIMES 2=RARELY 1=NEVER

____ 1. I'm willing to be specific, clear, and honest about what I will and won't be and do in a relationship.

____ 2. I'm willing to be specific, clear, and honest about what I want from others in relationships and specific situations.

____ 3. I'm willing to practice being a self-defining, non-anxious presence with others.

____ 4. I'm willing to honestly answer Jesus' question, "What do you want?"

____ 5. I'm aware of the toxic cookies that keep me from being specific, clear, and honest as I communicate with others.

____ 6. I can say "yes" and "no" with authority and integrity as others are specific, clear, and honest about what they want and need from me.

This Sound Check has a scale of 6 to 30. The closer your score is to 30, the more comfortable you are with making your requests and needs known in a direct and specific way. If your score is closer to 6, you may be leaving yourself open to being misunderstood or ignored. This may result in becoming resentful that others aren't treating you the way you want to be treated in relationships.

Morsels to Chew On

1. How do you respond to this quote by Theodore Geisel, aka Dr. Seuss: "Be who you are and say what you feel because the people who mind don't matter and the people who matter don't mind"?

2. Think of a relationship in which you want to be more yourself.

What will it mean to be a "self-defining, non-anxious, presence" in this relationship?

3. What would help you be more self-defining? Less anxious? More present?

4. What can be accomplished in the world as you state more clearly who you are and what you're about?

5. Recall a time when you asked for what you wanted and/or needed. Describe the situation in detail.

6. What are the three main reasons you don't ask for what you want or need? What's the payoff for not asking for what you want or need? What's the cost?

7. Why is it in everyone's best interest for you to speak up and ask for what you require or desire?

8. Describe a time when you should have said yes but said no. Then describe a time when you should have said no but said yes. Now describe a time when you said exactly what you needed to say. How do they differ in what you felt and accomplished?

9. What is your Divine Assignment? How can knowing this help you communicate more clearly and dive more deeply into partnership with God?

Dear God, you are straightforward about your love for me. You are clear about how I can stay connected to you. In fact, you share what you hope and dream for me as I live in and impact the world with you.

Forgive me for making things more difficult for myself and for others by not being clear about who I am, what I need, what I desire, and what I will say yes and no to. Fill me with your Spirit so I may be happily honest and forthright with myself, with you, and with my community. Help me work through whatever barriers I have, whether they be fear, false beliefs, anxious motives, or a misplaced sense of self-depreciation.

Reveal to me a clearer vision of what can happen in and around me as I seek to be more clear, direct, and wise in my communication.

In Christ's name, amen.

I believe that a simple and unassuming manner of life is best for everyone, best both for the body and the mind.

Albert Einstein

6

Your Lenses Make the Difference

The art of living lies less in eliminating our troubles than in growing with them.

Bernard M. Baruch

Conflict. Usually when we think about issues in communication, we think about conflict...about the people who drive us crazy, who don't listen, who we can't talk to, who are annoying.

Conflict has gotten a bad reputation, actually. We tend to think of it as war. But the truth is that whenever there are two or more people sharing space, thoughts, projects, meals, or resources, there will be conflict. None of us is exactly like another, so there will be differences. And this makes conflict inevitable.

Conflict is desirable at times. Working through issues can be productive and healthy in family and work relationships. Deeper intimacy in friendships and groups occurs as conflicts are addressed. In fact, avoiding conflict can produce more stress in the long run. The difference between growth and destruction is the level of maturity, love, and wisdom a person brings to his or her understanding of and willingness to resolve conflict. Conflicts have the potential to lead people to the hopes and dreams God has for his creation: redemption, forgiveness, resolution, intimacy, justice, and compassion. Conflict is not always bad; how we approach, handle, and deal with it can be.

Why Are We Fighting?

Generally there are three basic sources of conflict—the three P's of conflict:

Purpose. Remember Realities 1 and 2 in chapter 1? In a conflict of purpose, you and I don't agree on what's important. Because we each have different perspectives, conflicts of purpose are very common. You may think having dinner at six o'clock every night is important. I may think relaxing into the evening is important so whenever dinner gets on the table is just fine. Values, attitudes, and expectations are at the top of the conflict list in this category. How and why rules are established and enforced is significantly influenced by purpose and perspective.

Looking at most conflicts, we'll be able to see resolutions more quickly if we start with this diagnostic question right off the bat: "What's important to you that isn't being honored in this situation?" Ask your conflict partner this with an open heart, and you'll be well on your way to resolution.

Practice. Conflicts also arise when someone's behavior or speech clashes with what we want. Perhaps someone has a habit or verbal expression you find annoying at best and downright offensive or disgusting at worst. Maybe there are habits from your partner's family that just don't mesh with practices from your own. Practice conflicts are often the first sign there's a purpose conflict as well.

Personality. We each have our own personality or temperament. One aspect of our personality is our set of preferences on how we approach the world. One of the most well-known measurements of temperament is called the Myers-Briggs Type Indicator, or MBTI® for short. You can get a thumbnail sketch of your temperament measured by four scales if you go to www.personalitypathways.com. Once you get a picture of your temperament, you might find that some of the conflicts you have with others are simply a matter of temperament or preference.

The first scale, commonly known as the Introvert–Extravert, measures where you get and spend energy. This preference tells you why you feel energized in some situations and why you feel tired in others. An Extravert picks up steam the longer they spend time with others. They are gradually depleted the longer they have to spend time alone or in quiet. The Introvert is just the opposite. You can see why these two preferences might disagree on how to spend a Friday night together.

The second scale, the Sensing–Intuitive, measures how you pick up, understand, and organize information. Someone with a Sensing preference will be more in tune with the concrete, specific world of his or her sensory experiences. They focus on the here and now. An individual with an Intuitive preference will usually be looking at the overall possibilities of patterns and connections. He or she will tend to have an imaginative focus on the future.

The Thinking–Feeling scale measures the way a person prefers to make decisions and choices. A Thinking preference analyzes information in a detached way, looking at logic, facts, and principles when making a decision that will impact a situation. A Feeling preference will use a more subjective approach, looking at the impact on feelings, likes and dislikes, and needs and reactions. As you can imagine, one preference may tend to see the other as hard-hearted, while the opposite view sees the partner as too soft.

The Perceiving–Judging scale measures how someone prefers to take action in the world. Someone with a Perceiving preference gathers lots of information before making a decision or taking action. He would rather investigate first and act or decide later. Someone with a Judging preference tends to act or decide first and investigate later (if need be). This preference scale explains why we like shopping with some people and don't like shopping with others.

Understanding these scales and preferences can diffuse a great deal of conflict in any type of relationship, whether parent/child, work related, friendship, or romantic. For example, my dear husband and I are very closely matched on three of the temperament scales, but we're quite different on one scale. If we didn't know this, we could attribute all kinds of malicious, undermining behavior to each other, believing the other was trying to be stubborn and drive the other crazy.

On the last scale, the one that measures how you make decisions, my sweetheart is one who gathers lots of information, gathers more information, and then gathers just a little bit more before he makes a decision. I, on the other hand, make quick decisions and fix the problems made by those decisions afterward, if need be. Here's our classic illustration.

When my husband and I were building our second house together, we had enough experience with each other to know it would be very frustrating to both go to the design center for the first round of fixture choices. He would want to look at every sample of every cabinet, lighting, carpet, paint, and hardware the design center had. I would look at the options board, choose one, and be done with it.

So we decided he would go to the design center and take as long as he wanted to look at every option. He really enjoys that and I don't. Once he chose his top options, I would go with him for the final selections. Even that made me a little antsy, but it certainly worked better than if we didn't understand our differing styles!

David doesn't take a long time to decide something just to drive me crazy. And I don't make quick decisions out of disrespect to him. It's just the way we're wired.

The sooner we know things like this about our relationships, the better.

Why Exactly Do We Disagree?

A poll on the Internet site www.queendom.com (2/14/07) revealed what men and women cite as the most frequent reasons they argue. Women said the topics broke down like this:

Stress/fatigue	33.78%
Jealousy	14.95%
Money	14.82%
None—we never argue	9.54%
Chores	8.38%
Friends	6.25%
In-laws and extended family	5.15%
Parenting disagreements	4.70%
Infidelity	2.38%

For men the percentages looked like this:

Stress/fatigue	31.99%
Money	14.89%
None—we never argue	12.56%
Jealousy	12.17%
Chores	8.03%
Friends	5.95%
Parenting disagreements	5.82%
In-laws and extended family	4.79%
Infidelity	3.75%

Couples argue less because of the topic and more because of a state of mind or energy level. The most frequently cited reason a couple argues is because they are tired or feeling the pressures of life. Knowing this gives us a great big clue as to what we can do to decrease the level of conflict in our lives.

Differences of gender, culture, and age also contribute to conflict. Volumes have been written about the differences in the way men and women communicate, so I won't go into that deeply. And I do hesitate to stereotype. In my family the "typical" male and female patterns of communication are rather reversed. Yet researchers and social scientists have found some compelling patterns that do influence communication between genders.

The whole scenario of getting lost and asking for directions has practically become a cultural icon. It's the example used on many occasions to illustrate a pattern. A couple is late for a dinner date. The woman would like to stop and get directions because that will facilitate community on several levels. The man would not like to stop for directions as it is a sign of weakness and indicates a failure in competition. Yes, there is going to be conflict in that car.

Culturally we run into conflict when we don't understand the facial expressions, customs, speech patterns, and values of the family that just moved down the street. Cultural differences can even be found between people from different sides of the same town. These differences show up between economic classes, educational levels, and religious backgrounds. Even within the Christian community we have plenty of conflicts, and that's under the umbrella of being followers of Jesus Christ!

Age is one of the most potentially amusing differences that leads to conflict. Some students in a public speaking class I teach were talking about their "Peeps" in speeches. To me, Peeps are the charming little marshmallow creatures that show up in my Easter basket every spring. I had no idea college students were so into these yummy goodies. Come to find out, after exposing myself as a dinosaur, that "Peeps" are the circle of friends one hangs out with. Age is one of the most entertaining differences if handled with great grace, flexibility, and humor.

"CONFLICT" SOUND CHECK

The way we think about conflict has a profound effect on how we approach, weather, and use it. Respond to each statement using the following scale:

5=ALWAYS 4=OFTEN 3=SOMETIMES 2=RARELY 1=NEVER

____ 1. I view conflict as a fact of life.

____ 2. I view conflict as desirable.

____ 3. I understand I will, at times, be in conflict with someone over values, attitudes, and expectations.

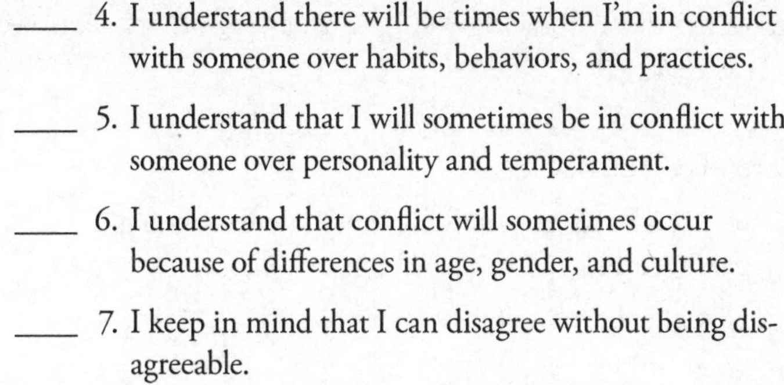

____ 4. I understand there will be times when I'm in conflict with someone over habits, behaviors, and practices.

____ 5. I understand that I will sometimes be in conflict with someone over personality and temperament.

____ 6. I understand that conflict will sometimes occur because of differences in age, gender, and culture.

____ 7. I keep in mind that I can disagree without being disagreeable.

How are you with conflict? If your score is closer to 35, you're probably comfortable with conflict and know it isn't a threat to you or your relationships. If your score is lower, what beliefs about conflicts need to be modified so you can view conflicts as opportunities for growth?

Understand Disagreement

One notion that came up time and again when I asked noted communicators about their thoughts on wise conflict was this: disagree without being disagreeable. We are each going to have our own opinion. The true measure of a good communicator, of a person who is going to be listened to, nice to talk to, and have the best chance of making a positive impact on the world, is someone who knows people are always more important than a topic or issue. A very smart pastor of mine, Dr. Bill Enright, was noted for saying, "I care less about where you come down on an issue than I do about how you treat each other in the process of the conversation."

Just because someone disagrees with us doesn't mean they disrespect us or our position. Conflict is inevitable, remember? Jesus didn't say we had to agree on all topics, but he was praying for our unity in spirit and in love (John 17:21-23).

The lenses through which you see the world are exclusive to you. No one else on the entire planet has the same prescription you do. God, the master designer, knows why that needs to be. Understanding and embracing our individual uniqueness is a huge step of maturity.

Understanding and embracing the uniqueness of others is an even larger step of maturity.

So...

...conflict is inevitable.

...conflict is fertile ground for increased understanding, growth, and love.

...let's make the most of it.

In the next chapter we'll look at some of the best time-tested practices to use when addressing conflict. We'll also examine a five-step process for resolving conflict in long-term relationships.

MORSELS TO CHEW ON

1. When you hear the word "conflict," what thoughts, images, and feelings come to mind?

2. How do you respond to the assertion that conflict itself is not good or bad, but how we respond to it brings positive or negative outcomes?

3. Think of the last several conflicts you've had with someone in particular. Were they conflicts of purpose, practice, or personality? Will pinpointing the cause help you choose a means of resolution for next time? Explain.

4. What type of personality preference do you have on the MBTI® scale? How might your preference be in conflict with someone you love? How can knowing this make a difference in your relationship?

5. As you consider the top reasons men and women alike say they have conflict with their partners (stress and fatigue), how does this shed light on the conflicts in your most important relationships?

6. Are you in a conflict that is primarily gender based? Culturally based? Age based? How will understanding conflict in light of these differences affect the way you approach the conflict?

Gracious God, in your wisdom you created everyone else on the planet different from me. Because of these differences, conflict is inevitable. I confess that I don't always see conflict as the breeding grounds for positive communication, community building, redemption, and growth. I often see conflict as a means to make someone else see things my way or someone's attempt to make me feel inferior.

Help me stay open to what I can do to view conflict in a positive way and work for a good outcome when it arises. Thank you.

In Christ's name, amen.

Can it be that man is essentially a being who loves to conquer difficulties, a creature whose function is to solve problems?

Gorham Munson

7

Give Peace a Fighting Chance

There is only one thing better than making a new friend, and that is keeping an old one.

Elmer G. Leterman

To be successful in resolving conflict, we have to *want* it to be resolved. That means we search our hearts and decide that our relationship with the other person is more important than continuing to be in active combat or in a cold war. Be honest. Sometimes we want to continue a fight to display power, hold out until we get what we want, punish someone else, or put distance between ourselves and the other person. We need to be very clear about our motives for continuing a conflict and decide, in light of our desire to join God in his hopes and dreams for creation, what we need to do to ease the conflict.

Let's dive into some of the best ways to approach conflict to achieve positive outcomes and strengthened relationships.

Get a Clear Picture

In Stephen Covey's landmark work *The Seven Habits of Highly Successful People,* Habit #5 is "Seek first to understand, then to be understood," which echoes part of a prayer attributed to St. Francis of Assisi:

O Divine Master, grant
that I may not
so much seek to be
consoled as to console;
to be understood as to
understand;
to be loved as to love;
for it is in giving that we
receive;
it is in pardoning that we
are pardoned;
and it is in dying that we
are born to Eternal Life.

Habit #5 is so important in fact, that Covey says, "If I were to summarize in one sentence the single most important principle I have learned in the field of interpersonal relations, it would be this: *Seek first to understand, then to be understood.* This principle is the key to effective interpersonal communication. Communication is the most important skill in life."[1]

Covey points out that employing this important key will actually cause most of us to have a fundamental shift in the way we view communication. "We typically seek first to be understood. Most people do not listen with the intent to understand; they listen with the intent to reply. They're either speaking or preparing to speak. They're filtering everything through their own paradigms, reading their autobiography into other people's lives."[2]

In conflict, it's helpful to remember that things are not always as we believe they appear. So how do we get a clearer picture? First we need to remember we may not be seeing things accurately. This takes humility and, oftentimes, a sense of humor.

I had a situation in which I was really glad I got the full picture before I reacted. My friend Missy and I were driving home from a writer and speaker's workshop when we decided to stop at a fast-food drive-through. I ordered our food and pulled up to the window, waiting to pay and receive our food. Now this particular establishment is not typically as quick as others, and the attendant gave us our drinks and straws first. As I hit my straw against the steering wheel to get the paper off, the guy behind me started beeping his horn. Soon I felt a little annoyed. *What does he want? What am I supposed to do?* I finally muttered something under my breath that only Missy could hear as I looked rather peevishly in the rearview mirror.

Missy laughed and said, "You goof! That's *you* beeping your own horn when you hit the steering wheel with your straw."

Oops! I was very glad I didn't get too far into my uppity little snit before I got the whole picture. And I was really glad I didn't give the gentleman behind me a dirty look!

Next we need to listen—really listen. Although we have a chapter coming up devoted to listening, it bears repeating when it comes to good conflict management and resolution.

My therapist husband has taught me a powerful phrase that is very helpful in especially emotional situations: "Is there anything else?" Tone of voice has a lot to do with the effectiveness of this question in diffusing negative emotions. If you let out a huffy sigh and put your hands on your hips while you're tapping your foot, you'll convey a completely different message than if you look your partner in the eye and make the inquiry in a genuinely interested voice. Remember, we're far more inclined to believe someone's nonverbals than his or her verbals.

Asking, "Is there anything else?" accomplishes three things. First, it signals to the other person, if done authentically, that we really are interested in hearing his whole story. Second, it helps us focus on truly listening. Third, it helps us gather more information that may be important to seeing the big picture.

Other characteristics of empathic listening include:

- We do *not* know exactly how another person feels, no matter how similar their situation is to ours. Resist the impulse to say "I know how you feel."

- Eye contact is important. It's especially important in empathic listening because we're not just picking up words, we're seeking to truly understand posture, facial expressions, hand movements, and general demeanor.
- This is not "active" or "reflective" listening. It's the deepest kind of listening we can do. We are truly absorbing someone else's concerns, perspective, and needs without making any kind of judgment or preconceived decision about that person.
- Only people who have a good handle on their own internal worlds (see chapter 3) can participate fully in empathic listening. Otherwise there's too much "noise" going on inside to really give space for the other person's communication to be received.

Those who practice empathic listening can do so because they know there's another part to Covey's habit..."to be understood." Covey's belief is that we can only really be understood by someone else when we have first sought to understand. Why? Because we will then be able to truly speak the person's language. When we listen enough to someone else's language, we know how to communicate in a way that makes sense to him, and he can more fully understand us.

Resist Manipulation

Conflict and its resolution often have to do with power. And power is not the same as influence. Power is the ability to make other people do what you want them to do. Power is the ability and authority to make a decision. In the world's terms, the person who is perceived to have greater status or prestige, who has the least to lose in a relationship, is the one with the greater power. But power can have negative expressions that break down the fabric of a community. This is often expressed by a winner–loser mentality, which is not an expression of justice, compassion, and equality. Some common negative expressions of power are:

- *Withdrawal.* We'll take a look at withdrawal more completely in chapter 14. Withdrawal is refusing to speak to the other person in the conflict because you are punishing or manipulating him.
- *Guilt production.* Some of the greatest guilt inducing questions start with, "How could you…?"
- *Deception.* When we do things behind another person's back to injure him or make a situation worse without telling him, we're using deception as power to blindside or ambush him.
- *Blackmail.* There is financial blackmail, of course, but emotional or mental blackmail can be just as powerful. When we are threatened with the disclosure of material we don't want others to know about unless we comply with someone else's demands, we are being blackmailed in a relationship.
- *Physical abuse and verbal threats.* Sixty percent of all marriages in the United States report some type of abuse. Abuse is all about power. The most common verbal forms are intimidation, threat, blaming, and humiliation. Consider this tactic I learned about from a friend. He said his uncle was not a tactful man. When an employee sat with him to ask for a raise, he placed a laughing box on the desk and told the employee after several seconds of laughter that he or she would not get an increase. Relationships were certainly affected in this exchange.
- *Criticism.* This form of power uses demeaning words to make another person feel worthless, thereby increasing his emotional dependence and increasing the power of the criticizer.

Manipulation can be harsh. Healthy people resist using power to get their way, and healthy people resist being manipulated. Power can disintegrate relationships.

Influence, on the other hand, is built on trust, reasonability, and relationship. Influence means we put the other person's best interests on the same level as what we hope to accomplish. People who seek influence are pleasant with others and have learned the fine art of negotiation. Influence means, at the very height of its perfection, that what we hope to accomplish is in the best interests of all we meet. That takes *time* to achieve. The difference between power and influence can be described in Proverbs 13:10: "Arrogant know-it-alls stir up discord, but wise men and women listen to each other's counsel" (MSG). Power produces instant results; influence tends to be more subtle but contributes more to relationship building.

"MAKING PEACE" SOUND CHECK

Being able to handle conflict well is foundational to changing your world for good with your communication. Respond to the following statements using this scale:

5=ALWAYS 4=OFTEN 3=SOMETIMES 2=RARELY 1=NEVER

____ 1. I seek first to understand, and then to be understood.

____ 2. In conflict, I remember I need to get a clear picture of what's happening with the person(s) I'm in conflict with.

____ 3. I use phrases such as "Is there anything else?" to draw out the other person and get a better understanding of what he or she is feeling.

____ 4. I recognize negative expressions of power, such as the silent treatment or inducing guilt, and avoid them. I use positive approaches involving good communication instead.

____ 5. I can clearly identify problems and be clear about what I want to see in the relationship or situation.

____ 6. I listen to the other person's perspective with clarity and empathy.

____ 7. I seek win–win solutions.

____ 8. I remember that each person in the conflict, including me, is a child of God.

If your score is close to 40, you're probably wonderful in conflict and can manage many types of disagreements and differences. You tend to be calm in conflict, able to think clearly, and not threatened by strong conflicting ideas and opinions. If your score is closer to 8, you might benefit from taking the focus off yourself in conflicts and looking more steadily at another's point of view and what's best for the good of the relationship.

Count to Ten

It's a mystery to me, but the topic of basketball coaches always comes up when talking about keeping one's cool and counting to ten when there's potential for a conflict. It could be because I'm from Indiana, and we have one very famous hothead in our Indiana basketball history. And basketball came up again when I asked my friends what it meant to them to keep their tempers when situations get heated. A long-time family friend, Laura, who coached my sister in basketball said, "I always could [maintain an even keel] because people don't listen to wild, ranting people. I always stayed calm while coaching basketball so the kids would learn by example what it means to stay calm and do what they had to do in any sticky situation. I never threw clipboards."

"Hot tempers start fights; a calm, cool spirit keeps the peace" (Proverbs 15:18 MSG). "A gentle answer turns away wrath, but a harsh word stirs up anger" (Proverbs 15:1). While it seems like an old-fashioned remedy, the cool spirit that produces gentle answers is often found in a person who has simply counted to ten. At the beginning of the countdown, someone may be ready to let someone have it, but then he takes the moments needed to respond in a beneficial manner. As

Henry David Thoreau said, "Nothing can be more useful to you than a determination not to be hurried." This determination means it's your right and your responsibility to take time to count to ten when you sense the water getting hotter in the relational teakettle.

Take a Laugh Break

Sara Davidson said, "The ability to laugh at life is right at the top, with love and communication, in the hierarchy of our needs." Sometimes our approach to conflict uses a little humor to diffuse the situation. I don't know if you've experienced this, but there are times when I'm in the middle of a conflict with my teenager and we're looking at each other intently. (OK, it's a stare-down.) Suddenly we both burst into laughter. At that moment of grace we realize we're taking something way too seriously, and the issue at hand is not worth a negative outcome.

We need to be wise, loving, and judicious when introducing humor into the resolution of conflicts. Humor can be used as a defense mechanism by avoiding taking anything seriously, which won't get us anywhere in the long run. We can also use humor inappropriately to put the other person down in ways that aren't really funny to him or her. But with discernment we can often tell when it's time for a laugh break or when a bit of humor will shed a broader light on the issues and the ongoing relationship.

Beth is one of the calmest people I know. But even she had her moments in the midst of a very large renovation project:

> We are remodeling our home. Extensively. And forever! The question about humor in conflict fits right into my remodel life. Humor has been critical to building a good relationship with my builder and his guys. Case in point is last week when we had a slab of granite delivered to create a desk for Don. The installers asked a question I couldn't answer immediately. I called Don, and thus ensued a long conversation about the location of a hole in this slab for computer wires and such. On and on and on Don went. I was getting

> exasperated so you can imagine how the waiting crew felt. I was trying to describe things, and Don was trying to imagine. Our builder finally said to just cut Don's legs off so he wouldn't have these wires all over his lap and everything would work out fine. It was a joke, so I finished it off by telling the granite crew leader, "See how Pat solves all of our problems? By the time this project is finished, we're going to be an inch tall!" The guy laughed and laughed, which bought me ten more minutes to get things finalized. Plus, now I have a running joke with Pat that will, I'm sure, help us out in the future.

Laughter has positive effects on our brains by stimulating neurotransmitters that help us relax, enabling a new perspective. As Lin Yutang said, "This I conceive to be the chemical function of laughter: to change the character of our thought."

No Name Calling

On the playground of life we're ill-advised to call someone names. You may hurt someone else, and you will certainly get yourself in trouble. Jesus was pretty clear about this: "Carelessly call a brother 'idiot!' and you just might find yourself hauled into court. Thoughtlessly yell 'stupid!' at a sister and you are on the brink of hellfire. The simple moral fact is that words kill" (Matthew 5:22 MSG).

Heather offers sound advice that honors a wise vow: My husband and I made a promise to each other that we would never resort to name calling or ugly words if we were upset with each other. The promise was simple at the beginning of our relationship, but it has proven valuable in that we remain respectful to each other even if we aren't happy with each other."

Friendships, romances, partnerships, parent/child and sibling relationships are hopefully sturdy, yet they can have their sensitive moments. Randolph Bourne observed, "Good friendships are fragile things and require as much care as any other fragile and precious thing." Name calling is not care giving.

Keep the Lid On

When you're riled by a situation or a person, the contrast given in Proverbs 29:11 comes to full bloom: "A fool gives full vent to his anger, but a wise man keeps himself under control." I had an opportunity to witness the contrast firsthand as I was traveling to a conference.

I flew to this particular conference. As I sat in the Chicago airport, I heard trouble brewing over my right shoulder. A husband and wife had deplaned and apparently he needed a wheelchair to get to their next destination in the airport. They were not happy that one had not been provided at the gate. They stood together for a little while, grousing a little bit. The wife decided to approach three airline employees who were standing close by. I heard the wife say to one of the employees, a woman who looked like she had probably been with the airline a fair number of years and had heard her share of customer grousing, "My husband should have been met here with a wheelchair. Who do I yell at so we can get one?"

Firmly but kindly the employee said, "Well, first of all, I suggest you don't yell at anyone. Then we'll walk over to this counter and call one over for you. I'm sorry it wasn't here to meet you, but we'll get that taken care of right away. You'll probably have more success if you ask nicely."

I about fell off my seat. What a great 30-second lesson in human relations!

Shortly after this incident my husband sent me one of those little emails with fun (but questionable) facts. The very first one said, "If you yelled for 8 years, 7 months, and 6 days, you would produce enough sound energy to heat one cup of coffee. (Hardly seems worth it.)"

My friend Heather makes me smile with the forthright way she expresses what it means to her to think before she speaks:

> Using appropriate words has been a goal of ours in our marriage and raising our children. I use a phrase with my oldest daughter that rings true here too: nice words or no words. I've found that if hateful words are pouring out of my mouth, I've likely not taken the time to think before I have spoken. I don't

> care who you are, that will get you in trouble. So I have to ask myself, "Who's in charge of my mouth? Satan or God?"

As an experiment for one month, try taking a deep breath, lowering your voice, and softening your eyes every time you feel the emotional kettle brewing. See if that facilitates better understanding between all involved.

Stay on Topic

When a conflict gets particularly lively, it can be very tempting to get off topic to diffuse some of the intensity. Two off-topic tactics to avoid are:

1. *Gunnysacking.* A gunnysack is an old-fashioned term for a big bag made of coarse fabric, such as burlap. People stuffed things into gunnysacks, maybe to be brought out at a later time, maybe to be thrown into the cellar. But they were large storage bags that held a lot of stuff. If you gunnysack someone in a conflict, you've been storing grudges for quite some time and choose to dump all their past misdeeds (real or imagined) all over them every time you have a conflict. It's a great way to avoid the real issue at hand.
2. *Branching.* Just as a tree trunk has branches, a conflict topic can have tempting side issues. But when we branch off into one of those issues, we are getting off topic. This makes our conflicts appear larger and more overwhelming than they actually might be. And it lessens the chance that a good and wise resolution can be reached for the current issue.

So if you're in conflict about who cooks and who cleans up the kitchen, stay on that topic until a resolution has been reached. *Then* you can start down the trail of who owns the remote control on Wednesday nights.

Request a Recess

A perfectly reasonable request is to ask for a 24-hour break if the subject is getting too emotional to talk about. This request must be an honest plea for cooling off or thinking time and not a stall in the hope the other person will let the issue slide. Set a definite time when you will come back together to calmly look at the issue again. Use the interim time to map out some thoughts using the "Five Specific Steps to Conflict Resolution" at the end of this chapter.

Honor Stress Levels

Remember the poll results in the last chapter? Most people cite stress and fatigue as the major reason they have conflicts with their partners. Fatigue, hunger, confusion, pain, and stress can cause us to be cranky and more prone to conflict than if we're rested, fed, sane, comfortable, and calm. So recognize this and avoid situations that can be fertile conflict breeding grounds.

1. Don't begin a heated discussion late at night.
2. Expect hungry children (and adults) to be more conflict oriented.
3. Choose a time for discussion that isn't going to be pressured by other obligations.
4. Set a sensory-rich stage for potentially tense conversations. For example, have music available that both parties enjoy. Light some aromatic candles in scents that have been shown to ease tension, such as lavender or green tea. Turn off electronics that could distract.
5. Spend a few quiet minutes in prayer so you can genuinely smile at your partner before the conversation begins.

Taking a Tone

You've seen it in your own life. When you're provoked you count to ten and speak gently to your provoker, and the confrontation is more likely to be resolved than if you answer quickly in a harsh tone. Speaking gently as a regular habit dramatically alters everyday interactions as those around us realize we're not to be feared or dismissed because of a gruff or loud nature. We are more likely to be received well by others and more likely to be heard when we use gentle ways and kind words.

When I present this particular aspect of having a smart mouth in a seminar or retreat, I receive skeptical looks from the audience, many of whom have read books on assertiveness and getting what you want by speaking up and asking. We can be assertive and forthcoming about our feelings, opinions, and instructions. But Scripture does suggest that we never speak before we have assessed as much of the situation as we can, that we use a kind and gentle tone over a harsh and angry one, and that we make our responses short and sweet and worth hearing. We can convey the same words in a variety of tones with a predictable variety of results.

Five Specific Steps to Conflict Resolution

This process is a concrete and methodical way to work through a conflict. Entering into this process assumes that people in the conflict want to work things through. It is essential to remember the basic principles found in chapters 1 through 4 that established what it takes to be a wise, loving, and mature person in communication:

- Realize you and your partner are each coming from your own perspective.
- Establish and maintain trust through loving honesty.
- Keep your self-talk healthy and loving.
- Be determined to listen well.

Now, let's examine the five steps to conflict resolution.

1. *Identify the problem.* The problem shows itself as something that happens over and over, and it is disturbing to at least one person in the conflict.

2. *Be clear about the new behaviors you would like to see in the relationship.* You may have a disagreement with your son and daughter over the way they address you in the morning when everyone is in a hurry to get out the door to school or to work. Perhaps you have fallen into patterns in which family members stay in bed until the last minute, don't prepare bags and clothes the night before, and expect other family members to read their minds about what they need to get ready. Your children may have become increasingly snappy and rude in the way they talk to you.

When you are working through these steps, be specific about the new behaviors you want, along with the ones you don't want.

3. *Identify thought patterns that might need to change.* While some behaviors do indeed need to change, there are also times when how we think about a situation can lessen the conflict. We may come to a new awareness about the other person or ourselves that enables us to take a less offended or defended position in the conflict.

4. *Be able to articulate your partner's position with clarity and empathy.* This takes time and intentionality. It takes a selfless approach to hear what your partner is saying and to accurately feed back to him or her what is being said and not what you think you hear or what you want to hear.

5. *Employ the essence of good conflict resolution called "win–win."*

> It is imperative to look for win–win solutions to conflicts. Solutions in which one person wins and the other person loses mean that one person is not getting his or her needs met. As a result, the person who loses may develop feelings of resentment, anger, hurt, and hostility toward the winner and may even look for ways to get even. In this way, the winner is also a loser. In intimate relationships, one winner really means two losers.[3]

Designing win–win solutions takes a mature ability to get a big-picture view of the situation and the relationship. You and your partner can brainstorm potential solutions without initially evaluating what's tossed out. You get as many ideas on paper as you can. Nobody is allowed to say "That won't work because..." or "That's a stupid idea..."

Once you have a list of possible solutions in which each partner would gain something from the outcome, evaluate the options with these questions:

- Does the solution satisfy both individuals? (Is it a win–win solution?)
- Is the solution specific? Does it specify exactly who is to do what, how, and when?
- Is the solution realistic? Can both parties realistically follow through with what they have agreed to do?
- Does the solution prevent the problem from recurring?
- Does the solution specify what is to happen if the problem recurs?[4]

Remember Who You Are

Remember Beth who was in the midst of a remodeling project? She gets it when it comes to influence that will be felt today and for years to come.

> I have had many opportunities to "get hot" about details I never dreamed mattered. But, at least to my way of thinking, I haven't once felt angry with anyone, let alone shown any anger. And there have been times when it would have been expected, believe me. The reason is simple: I set the tone for my home and for my family. Anger just isn't necessary. We chose a reasonable and trustworthy builder, and while he and I have had conversations about things, they are exchanges of information that we then each have to digest. Sometimes I have to see that he is right and vice versa. But if I ever let myself get hot, I consider my family's reputation, my children's attitude about this remodel, and the tension

> increasing in my home. And that's not even considering the effect on the builder and his crew. You can bet I pray every evening, giving gratitude for another day's progress and pray every morning for strength, courage, and the right words to say to get us through another day of noise and mess. I'm no saint, but Andy (our standard poodle) and I are making it through each day!

Conflict is indeed inevitable. But the positive or negative nature of conflict is not in the problem itself but in what we choose to believe about it, how we choose to approach it, how we choose to treat other people in the midst of it, and what we choose to believe God had in mind for its presence in the relationship.

Morsels to Chew On

1. What is difficult about seeking to understand before being understood? What could it ultimately do for you in your important relationships?

2. Which of the negative uses of power or manipulation have you experienced? Which have you used?

3. Rate the following conflict managers by how often you use them. Go from 1 to 10, with 1 being "Use Often" and 10 being "Use Seldom."

    __ Count to ten
    __ Laughter
    __ No name calling
    __ Keep emotions in check
    __ Stay on topic
    __ Request a recess
    __ Honor stress levels
    __ Gentle tone of voice

4. Reflect on your score. What are your strong suits when it comes to engaging in conflict? What do you bring to conflicts that increases the chance of a positive outcome and strengthened relationship? What do you need to improve to engage in conflict with redemptive possibilities?

5. Choose a conflict you are currently facing or one you anticipate. Clearly outline your approach using the Five Steps of Conflict Resolution. Share the Five Steps with the other person.

6. How might the encouragement to "remember who you are" make a difference the next time you are engaged in a conflict?

Dear God, thank you for giving me grace for each challenge I face. Help me remember I am your child and to be mindful of the rest of your children as we live together in community. Because we're each different, there will be conflict. But you weave our conflicts into more beautiful and durable cloth if we invite your Spirit to lead us.

Give me the presence of mind, tenderness of heart, and strength of self to stay involved with my brothers and sisters to work toward the world of your hopes and dreams.

In Christ's name, amen.

Happiness is not the absence of conflict, but the ability to cope with it.

ANONYMOUS

8

I Need to Tell You...

If you have some respect for people as they are,
you can be more effective in
helping them to become better than they are.

John W. Gardner

Giving and receiving correction, instruction, and constructive feedback are natural parts of our everyday relations with others. No matter where we are in years, career, or life position, we will certainly receive such communication. And no matter how inexperienced we are, we can always offer something to someone else. Communicating effectively and for good means we know how to give and receive wisely.

Feedback (critique) and instruction aren't the same and can be approached in different ways. They both are best given and received with healthy doses of respect for self and others. And what do you do when you have to be the bearer of bad news?

Create a Safe Atmosphere

The atmosphere has direct bearing on whether critique and instruction are received in positive or negative ways. Defensiveness sets one tone; supportiveness sets a completely different one.

Defensiveness occurs when the person being helped senses an attitude of harsh or nonsupportive evaluation or judgment on the part of the sharer. When correction includes blaming and fault-finding, a sense of attack causes most of us to instinctively put our guard up. Fight, flight, or submit seem to be our only options—none of which are helpful in building relationships and solving problems.

Supportiveness is fostered in an atmosphere of describing what we see, checking our observations with the other person, and coming up with doable solutions. This creates an atmosphere of acceptance, teamwork, and positive expectation.

Defensiveness will most certainly grow in an atmosphere where the person being corrected feels the critiquer is wielding their superiority over the other. The person feels threatened and put down. It's hard to stay engaged in a conversation when self-worth is threatened. A sense of mutual respect and equality, if only based on the fact that both people are children of God, each created in the image of God, emphasizes similarities rather than differences. Supportiveness in this dimension means we look for ways in which people can help one another. Even though a person may be in authority over another, correction comes with a positive, person-to-person communication.

Control also engenders defensiveness. Control indicates we know better than someone else how he ought to think or behave. When correction is delivered with an air of power, the other person is sure to shut down for protection. Communication is halted, and the situation goes downhill fast. Supportiveness, on the other hand, will focus on the situation and what can be done to work it through in a way that is most beneficial to all involved. We don't tell someone what should be done; we explore together what can be done.

And be careful to avoid manipulation. Using "spin," delivering partial information, laying traps, using trickery of any kind, produces immediate defensiveness because people feel controlled. Secretive strategy erodes trust. Spontaneity and relaxed delivery, on the other hand, keep the atmosphere lighter. You'll bring an unrehearsed, unhurried, possibly even humorous quality to the conflict. The lightheartedness needs to be delivered tactfully, especially in conflict situations.

While neutrality may seem like a good quality in conflict, it can actually act as a barrier that produces defensiveness. Conflict resolution works best in an environment of caring involvement with the other person. Neutrality stimulates aloofness. To build supportiveness, use empathy. Empathy is the ability to see things from the other person's point of view. Empathy says to another person, "Your perceptions, preferences, feelings, and needs are worth taking into consideration, even if they aren't the same as mine."

Defensiveness thrives in an atmosphere of certainty. When we are in a conflict with someone and indicate there is no need for more information, opinions, or discussions, the other person may feel cut off and left without influence or voice. This creates a hostile environment. When we perceive we are in a supportive situation in which minds and hearts stay open, people are better able and willing to listen, explore, and discuss.

❧ "Special Delivery" Sound Check ❧

When we're called to deliver critique or instruction, we'll be most effective if we set the stage and deliver our lines wisely. Respond to each statement using the following scale:

5=ALWAYS 4=OFTEN 3=SOMETIMES 2=RARELY 1=NEVER

____ 1. I set up an atmosphere of supportiveness before and when I give feedback or critique to someone.

____ 2. I combine kindness and truthfulness when I give feedback or critique.

____ 3. When critiquing or instructing others, I use words that are worth hearing and heeding.

____ 4. Before I give critique or instruction, I spend time listening for and to God's Spirit.

____ 5. I listen thoroughly to the other person before I give critique or instruction.

____ 6. I can tell the difference between someone who truly desires feedback and someone who is a chronic complainer.

____ 7. When I have to give unpleasant news, I do so with compassion and directness. I also make sure we're in a distraction-free environment.

If your score is closer to 35, you're probably someone people see as wise, compassionate, and worth listening to. You tend to deliver critique and instruction humanely. If your score is in the teens or lower, you could take a closer look at situations that require critique or instruction and see how you can be more effective and sensitive in your approach and speech so the recipient will be better able to hear and accept your information.

Giving Constructive Feedback

Now, when it comes to critique or feedback, some of us have no trouble telling what we perceive to be the truth. Those of us with this kind of temperament honestly believe the best thing we can do for someone is to point out what's wrong so the person can fix it. The only trouble with this approach to critical review is we sometimes leave in our wake a string of wounded hearts and bleeding souls because of our harsh approach. We would do well to heed the deep truth Paul spoke of in 1 Corinthians 13:10: "We know only a portion of the truth, and what we say about God is always incomplete. But when the Complete arrives, our incompletes will be canceled" (MSG). When tempted to tell the truth as we perceive it, we can all use a dose of perspective and humility. Don't assume incompetency. Instead use a gentle, supportive, "If you do this..." attitude.

On the other hand, some of us would be happy to tell the truth except we're afraid it might hurt somebody's feelings. Those of us with this kind of temperament wait until we can find something very positive in the situation, believing that bringing up people's strengths is the best thing. Yet in keeping a negative under wraps until we figure out a positive way to say something, we may let things slip through and continue to damage the situation or relationship.

Both the Old and the New Testaments share important advice regarding how to approach people. Proverbs 3:3 offers: "Do not let kindness and truth leave you; bind them around your neck, write them on the tablet of your heart" (NASB). The wisdom of the sage is echoed years later when Paul admonishes the church at Ephesus, "God wants us to grow up, to know the whole truth and tell it in love—like Christ in everything" (Ephesians 4:15 MSG).

Truth and love in perfect balance. One way to look at how these two relate is through color. My favorite color is purple, so I see the continuum like this.

True blue is the space where stark, raw, uncensored truth lives. If we share too much truth, we might decimate the person we're trying to help.

Sympathetic love lives in the Valentine red space. This is where great compassion, nurture, and understanding dwell. The drawback on this end is there may be too much affection and softness so we don't offer accountability or confrontation, which is necessary to help the person grow and change.

Speaking the truth in love merges true blue and Valentine red into beautiful shades of purple, which brings out the best in the person we're addressing. Let's face it, if someone blasts away at us, are we going to listen? If someone is too soft, will he or she make an impact and call us to our greatest version of ourselves as God created us? At our best, we each want to be lovingly challenged by people who know us, believe in us, and want the very best for us. Speaking the truth in love is the best form for criticism.

Work situations can be tricky. The following is a terrific example of how criticism can be done gently in memo form:

> At the risk of sounding like a former U.S. president, I'm writing to encourage us to be "kinder and gentler" to each other. As I've watched recent staff meetings and listened to encounters with and between customers, I've become really

> concerned with the tone and words we're using to address each other. In my time with our company, I've always found hope in our ability to address each other with kindness and respect, no matter how difficult or divisive the issue.
>
> Several years ago I was honored to be on a consulting team for one of my former employers. I was astonished to sit in staff meetings and witness the hostility and spitefulness with which co-workers addressed each other. I remember thinking, "This would never happen where I work now" and feeling glad to be a staff member in a place where people treated each other with respect and dignity.
>
> I fear that recently some of this philosophy has been lost or may be in danger of being lost. I ask that we remember to treat each other with dignity, generosity, and esteem, no matter how vast our differences and disagreements. I recognize that what I'm asking goes against the tide of incivility which is so prevalent in our culture today. However, if we lower our standards of mutual respect, civility, and kindness in conversation, we stand to lose much more than we are likely to win.

I asked the memo writer about the effect this note had on the people to whom it was written. He reports that it is now referred to, lovingly, as the "discourse" memo. He even received a particularly affirming response from one of his trusted and respected mentors. Following a critique with possible solutions keeps the feedback from sounding like a complaint. Complaints without potential solutions often dead-end or derail communication. In this situation the community was strengthened and relationships garnered more of the character God intends for his creation.

As we explored in chapter 3, speaking the truth in love will be easier if we start with ourselves. "We need to understand that our commitment to honesty, first and foremost, has to do with telling *ourselves* the truth—and telling the truth *about* ourselves."[1] When we practice telling the truth in love to ourselves, we can do it more easily with others. Because we neither overinflate ourselves nor beat ourselves into the ground, we can be real, gentle, honest, and sometimes even humorous with others.

In giving constructive feedback, Laura likes to combine an affirmation with a question that exposes her view on the situation. She likes to say, in essence, "I love you, and what do you think about this?" My husband says there's a key word in this sentence: "and." Most of us are tempted to use the word "but," which signals to the hearer that we're negating the phrase that came before it. When we use the word "but," the listener doesn't really hear the "I love you" part. He or she just hears the second part. Using "and" instead of "but" gives the listener the chance to process the whole intention of your communication.

Giving Instruction

We can be good instructors by following several key principles:

1. *Give actual instruction that is wise and nourishing.* Studying the book of Proverbs gave me such good ammunition with my children. Nearly every day I wanted to quote to them Proverbs 1:8-9: "Listen, my son, to your father's instruction and do not forsake your mother's teaching. They will be a garland to grace your head and a chain to adorn your neck." This sounded pretty good. I can always use more scriptural backing to make my motherly points. Then I realized with a sickening thud that a large part of Solomon's exhortation was based on the fact that I would be offering words of instruction that were worthy of hearing and heeding. As my children's instructor, I actually had to have something nourishing and wise to say.

What a blessing when I recognized Scripture has so much to say to help parents, teachers, grandparents, and other significant adults entrusted with children. There is a great deal of sound teaching for health in heart, soul, mind, and strength. (Proverbs chapter 4 provides a wonderful model of instruction offered by a parent.)

We can be people of wise instruction when we carefully consider the person to whom we are speaking and prayerfully ask the Holy Spirit to help us recall relevant scriptures and truth. Wisdom's promise resounds through Proverbs 3:6: "In all your ways acknowledge [the LORD] and he will make your paths straight." Hopefully you've experienced that wonderful sense after a conversation that you were simply the mouthpiece for God's instruction, admonition, or encouragement. "A word aptly spoken is like apples of gold in settings of silver" (25:11).

I've had the privilege of encountering many great instructors, but one stands out. When my writing and speaking were in infancy, I asked Dr. Jay Kesler, then president of Taylor University in Upland, Indiana (my alma mater), if I might have an hour of his valuable time to share my life vision so he could offer direction. During our visit he sat quietly while I articulated the ideas brewing in my soul. With great care and patience he listened, and then he said, "You know, I've been in prayer about what you're saying the whole time you've been talking so I could offer you wise counsel and direction." He'd prayed as he deeply listened. What a gift! As he offered his insights and musings, I felt the conversation was anointed by the Holy Spirit, and I knew I was the blessed recipient of wise instruction.

2. *Understand that a person is always more important than the lesson you have to share.* Proverbs offers wise insights to people who truly want to bring out the best in others: "Knowing what is right is like deep water in the heart; a wise person draws from the well within" (20:5). Wise instructors help others draw the answers they seek out of their hearts, out of their own selves. Wise instructors know solutions are only as good as they are genuine to the person with the problem. We help others by introducing them to their own wisdom. Benjamin Disraeli wisely observed, "The greatest good you can do for another is not just to share your own riches, but to reveal to him his own."

A deeply wise advisor is my former colleague Dr. Joan. With humor, unparalleled listening skills, and an ear for the "third voice" (the Holy Spirit) in every conversation, Joan has guided me through ideas and situations with great dexterity and wisdom. Whenever I have an idea for a project, seminar, or book, I go to Joan. She attends with great interest. And then she does the most amazing thing. By asking a series of questions and suggesting options I might want to consider, she helps me get a clearer picture of my path and my plan. Although she rarely gives direct instruction, she guides in a way that lets me know she trusts the unfolding of the Holy Spirit's wisdom in my life. She helps me be a better person because she values and believes in me. Wise instruction pays equal attention to the value of the person as well as to the value of the training.

Marilyn nominated one of her pastors for a Smart Mouth Award in the category of "Cultivating Wisdom Through Respect":

> My nominee for the 2007 Smart Mouth Award is Karen Lang, associate pastor at Second Presbyterian Church.
>
> I had an appointment with Karen in December of 2006. I was (and still am) going through a very difficult period in my life. I have made some choices that seem to have been led by God but also are causing me much anxiety and questioning as they unfold. In talking with Karen about these issues, I told her I had a theological question. I asked her if God would forgive me. I knew He would, but in some part of me I could not truly believe or feel that He would forgive.
>
> As I talked Karen listened, probed, and asked good questions so my story came pouring out with all the anger and pain. Finally Karen paused for a moment, looked at me, and said these smart words: "I think you are focusing too much on yourself. Instead, you should be focusing on the character of God."
>
> She then encouraged me to write down the characteristics of God as I studied Scripture and had daily devotional times. I must say that in the eight or so weeks since that time, my life has changed. I took her words to heart, and every time I read Scripture, I keep pen and paper handy. I now have a long list of the amazing, accepting, healing, and loving characteristics of God that I reread whenever I begin to fear or feel self-pity.
>
> Karen's words were truly God's message to me that day. To her and to Him I am deeply grateful.

This is wise speech to the highest degree. Rev. Lang pointed Marilyn in the direction of seeing her creator and herself in a more realistic way. Karen did something very important before she gave her feedback—she listened. She made sure she understood Marilyn before she steered her in a direction. Rev. Lang would not give the same answer to a different person or situation. In wisdom, she *listened* to Marilyn and to the Holy Spirit, and then gave instruction.

Nothing is more disheartening to the receiver and inauthentic on our part than slapping a "spiritual" solution on a situation before we've actually listened.

3. *Know the difference between people who truly want instruction and people who are not interested in solutions.* As wise instructors, we need to understand that people who come to us for instruction are responsible for their own growth. We've all encountered people in our lives who, over the course of time, showed they really didn't want the things they were complaining about to change. You can tell this has happened to you when you look at the caller ID on the phone, sigh, and decide you just don't have the energy to deal with that particular person right now.

As Christians many of us feel it's our obligation to make things better for others, to help them through pain. Unfortunately our healthy boundaries sometimes get blurred, and we get sucked into trying to make things better for someone who honestly doesn't want to become healthy, responsible, or mature. I'm not talking about someone temporarily disabled by grief, loss, or a large transition. Those can take months to work through, and a good friend can and will stand by.

I'm talking about complainers or people content with the status quo. I admit I struggle with the most helpful way to deal with this kind of instructional situation. So as I was preparing to write this section, I did what I recommend for times when you want to think something through—I consulted my "wisdom council"! I asked a team of Christian mental health and ministerial professionals what they do when they encounter a person who doesn't really want to change anything. Instead they just want to grouse.

Dr. Donna Lazarick, a psychologist and life coach, said "active listening" (see chapter 4) with a tiny bit of confrontation is good. Don't indulge the complainer in too much sympathy. She suggests a response like, "Wow, you have been frustrated about this for at least two years. It must be hard to figure out how to change." If the complaint is consistently about another person, Doc Donna might gently suggest, "The only person you can change is yourself."

She also observes that whiners usually don't want to do anything, so consistently and gently suggest they need to do something besides complain. Donna says changing the subject can be a good tactic too. As a last resort, the friendship might need to end.

A minister whose wisdom I respect told this very candid story about a situation an entire group of people faced in a congregation.

> There was a man in a church I served who always, *always* complained about everything. Things that didn't deserve his complaints got them anyway. Things that seemed fine, he found fault with. People tried and tried to help him, to show him sunshine, to show him how things could turn out better than he thought. All efforts failed. Nothing worked. I was one of those persons, thinking we could change him and make him happy. We thought we could arrest his complaining if we prayed enough, if we loved him unconditionally, if we all were sunshiny, positive, and optimistic.
>
> Here is what I and others learned from a psychologist: The person actually *liked* to complain and feel miserable. This was a radical concept to me. This person was very happy when he complained, when he was down in the dumps, when he seemed so very unhappy, when he found fault with things, others, his family.
>
> And here's another totally new concept for me: I was making things worse by trying to cheer him up. He didn't want to feel better. He didn't want me or anyone else to make things better or to show how things could get better. That *blew*

my mind. I felt, in fact, tricked. Since all behavior has benefits, has payoffs, we were asked to figure out what the benefits were to this man for complaining. And the reason was he'd found an invincible, solitary, and guarded position that no one could touch. He had identity. He could control outcomes. He found a way for persons to come to him, care for him, spend time with him hoping to make him feel better, yet he was unreachable. It was a puzzle. Even if they left frustrated and feeling like failures, this man felt fine feeling grumpy, critical, unhappy, and sad. That is the way he wanted it. No one could reach him. No one could change him. No one could influence him. He was impervious and imperious to any good thought, any good intention, any goodness at all.

Now he may not have known this as clearly as I have just stated it.

So here was our eventual action plan (it may sound cold-blooded): We left him alone. We created a distance. We didn't try to make him feel better. We didn't try to convince him there was another way to look at things. We didn't allow him to use our goodness, our time, and our best efforts to help him once we found out he didn't want to be helped. We left him to God, just like it says in the New Testament. We shook the dust off our feet (Matthew 10:14) and went on to the next person who yearned to be helped, to be loved, to have a good word, to get and feel better, the next person *who wanted good news.* We kept going with our gifts to the next person instead of wasting our precious gifts of love. We remembered the man was part of the body of Christ (1 Corinthians 12:12ff.), but he had to want to be an active part of the body instead of being a dismembered section. And when we walked away, he didn't miss us.

It was one of the toughest lessons I have ever learned.

Dr. Mary Schwendener-Holt reinforces what we're talking about: Communication is always a mix of our own perceptions, the other person's perceptions, and reliance on the remarkable presence of God's Holy Spirit:

I encounter people who don't want to be helped, who don't want to change, but it is hard to put my approach into words.

There are two sets of issues here—my issues and their issues.

My stuff—This is one of those situations where reminding myself that these people are *children of God* is the most helpful thing I can do. When I find myself annoyed (and the situation of complaining with no changing annoys me quickly), I can tap into my compassion (and what God wants me to do) more quickly if I start thinking about the people as individuals, "Scott/Lisa/Kathy—Child of God," in my head. It's amazing how quickly this turns my heart. Sometimes, if I'm really annoyed, I ask God to soften my heart. And it's also amazing how well this works. So first, I recognize and ask for God's help with my attitudes and feelings.

Their stuff—Once I've remembered they are children of God it gets a lot easier to deal with their issues. I generally work from the direction of:

1. It is hard (and not fun) to change.
2. It is more fun to complain and not change.
3. What is gained from staying the same?
4. What is so scary about changing?
5. What will be lost if you change?
6. It's OK to not change.
7. It's OK for me not to spend a lot of time listening to you not change, but I'm here if you want to do something besides complain.

I think questions 3, 4, and 5 get me on the same side of the fence with them. Then we can lean on the fence together and think about why they don't want to change (and be OK with that).

I have complaining boundaries—five minutes generally where you can complain, whine, gripe, etc. But if we're not

> going to do something about changing it, then we probably ought to both go our separate ways. Then, of course, I'll pray at stoplights, come to church on Sunday, put their names in my prayer requests, and wait for God to do his thing. I'm finding it is a whole lot easier to put these people in God's hands and kind of sit back, be there with the clients, and watch for the miracles.
>
> Once I put them in God's hands I also don't have to deal with my issues as much. I just need to be loving and compassionate while having boundaries and being aware that change is not fun and is generally scary. As we say in the addictions group I facilitate at the state hospital: If recovery were easy, we'd have done it already!

There are two important factors to remember when dealing with difficult people. As a psychology instructor at a community college, I have begun to understand and teach my students that people do things for what seems to them to be good and compelling reasons, whether it makes sense to others or not. We don't always understand why people do what they do, but from a behavioral point of view, people will most often repeat behavior that somehow has a positive payoff for them...or what they perceive to be a more positive payoff than changing their behavior. That's a pretty powerful dynamic in the way people function.

A second interesting lesson is that, as Christians, we may perceive that finally moving away—"abandoning" these people—seems cold-blooded. But really, what other healthy choice is there in the long run? Enabling does not ultimately heal a person who doesn't want to make healthy changes. Enabling eventually saps the energies that we could be using for good. As reported in the book of Luke:

> Later the Master selected seventy and sent them ahead of him in pairs to go to every town and place where he intended to go. He gave them this charge...
>
> "On your way! But be careful—this is hazardous work. You're like lambs in a wolf pack...

> "When you enter a home, greet the family, 'Peace.' If your greeting is received, then it's a good place to stay. But if it's not received, take it back and get out. Don't impose yourself...
>
> "When you enter a town and are not received, go out in the street and say, 'The only thing we got from you is the dirt on our feet, and we're giving it back. Did you have any idea that God's kingdom was right on your doorstep?' Sodom will have it better on Judgment Day than the town that rejects you" (10:1,3,5-6,10-12 MSG).

This is, without a doubt, one of those situations in which we need to be as innocent as doves and a wise as serpents as we believe the best of others yet know when we need to make adjustments in the level of involvement we have in trying to instruct, correct, and make suggestions for positive change (Matthew 10:16)

Yikes! I'm the Messenger of Bad News!

An article about communicating bad news began with this story:

> An artist asked the gallery how his paintings were selling.
>
> "I have some good news and some bad news," said the gallery owner. "A guy was in here yesterday and asked if your paintings will appreciate in value after your death. When I told him 'yes,' he bought all 15 of them!"
>
> "That's great!" said the artist. "But what could the bad news possibly be?"
>
> "He was your doctor."

This is a humorous example of a necessary truth: We are all called upon to deliver bad news at one time or another. Maybe we are business owners or managers who have to tell people they no longer have jobs. Perhaps we're teachers having to tell students and parents that work isn't getting done and grades aren't being maintained. We might be friends who have to tell other friends about the failing health of someone. People find themselves delivering spiritual, emotional, mental, physical, and social bad news as part of their job descriptions.

You might be a parent who has to explain why Rover or Fluffy isn't going to be roaming the house anymore.

Nobody likes bad news. Nobody wants to hear it; nobody wants to share it. So we sugarcoat and beat around the bush. Many times the bad news is as hard on us as on the person hearing the news. Bad news delivery calls for many of the threads we've examined in this book: honesty, directness, clarity, tact, and compassion. Janet Pederson offers these tips:

- Pick a time and place when you can be free of distraction or interruption.
- Get right to the point. Announce up front that you have some unpleasant, unfortunate, disappointing, or disturbing news. The right words? Simple: "I have some unpleasant news."
- Use "softeners" to open. For example: "I'm sorry to have to tell you..." or "I'm afraid that..."
- If the news is coming as a shock to the other person, be prepared for his or her emotional reactions. Let them vent, if they seem to need to. Do not try to get them to "calm down, be reasonable."
- Especially if you are in a workplace environment and are concerned about their reacting with violence, make sure you have provided for your own safety and security. Either have a witness present or alert security in advance.
- If appropriate, once the shock has abated offer the people resources they can pursue.
- Forgive yourself for being the bearer of bad news. You are not causing their distress...the news is.[2]

There will most certainly be times when you need to deliver feedback, instruction, or bad news. The Realities of chapter 1 will help as you address the other person with respect, the genuine love of God, and an eye for what's best for your recipient. When you know yourself and your own motives and perspectives, know the perceptions and background of the other person as well as you can, and rely on the very wise Spirit of God, you will be able to do your best.

Morsels to Chew On

1. In what situations and relationships are you called on to deliver critiques or feedback?

2. How can you build an environment of supportiveness when giving critiques or feedback?

3. Think of a situation in which you offered a critique or feedback. How did you do? What was the truth of the situation? Could you deliver this truth more lovingly now? How would you address the person and the issue truthfully and in love today?

4. Reflect on the difference between using "but" and "and" when offering feedback. Give examples.

5. How does prayer and asking good questions enable you to offer better instruction for others?

6. How can you use Janet Pederson's tips for delivering bad news the next time you are in that position?

Dear God, there are times when I offer critiques or instruction to others. Enable me to do it with a spirit of respect and honor. Give me a true desire to make a positive impact on someone else's life.

Help me remember to pray and be thoughtful in listening. Give me the right questions to ask so I may get a clearer picture of what the other person is experiencing and what he or she needs to grow.

When I'm called on to deliver bad news, give me insights and grace to do it well. I ask for discernment to know what I can offer as resources to the person who is receiving the bad news.

In all of these circumstances, give me your wisdom through the Holy Spirit.

In Christ's name, amen.

A helping word to one in trouble is often like a switch on a railroad track...an inch between a wreck and smooth, rolling prosperity.

Henry Ward Beecher

9

RECEIVING WITH GRACE

We have not passed the subtle line between childhood and adulthood until...we have stopped saying, "It got lost" and say, "I lost it."

SYDNEY J. HARRIS

Good communication is not only how you give but how you receive. Learning to distinguish between and deal appropriately with thoughtless criticism and helpful counsel will bring great insights and maturity to a person. Proverbs 12:1 says, "Whoever loves discipline loves knowledge, but he who hates correction is stupid." That's a pretty clear statement, isn't it!

We will most certainly face feedback, instruction, and bad news simply because we are part of the human community. Family members, friends, bosses, and even people we bump into in the grocery store give us feedback on a constant basis. Our response is influenced largely by our self-perception.

How do you respond to feedback? Do you answer from a solid core or are you more of a reactor based on external factors, stress, or unresolved issues? Randy, a sales professional, has been in a variety of work environments, Christian and non-Christian. I asked him for his perspective on how he handles constructive criticism in the workplace.

> Let's face it, receiving "constructive criticism" from our managers during reviews or throughout the week is just plain difficult, even if we know it is right on target and is being delivered in the most eloquent, tactful way. Our human tendency is to come away with that nagging feeling in the pit of our stomachs that we don't want to hear it or deal with it. Negativity may rise in us and make us want to lash out and not take responsibility. It is much easier to come up with myriad excuses and place blame on others rather than surrendering to the simple truth we know is there.
>
> The question is, How easy is it for us to hear truth about an area in our lives that needs to change?

Randy wisely noted in our correspondence that a famous king from the Old Testament was in the same position. The story of the prophet Nathan's rebuke of King David after David's adulterous, murderous behavior provides insight into what it means to accept critique—even harsh critique, as in David's case (2 Samuel 12:1-14).

David's response is simple and complete, "I have sinned against the LORD" (verse 12).

Randy has found that one way for him to effectively work with constructive criticism is to listen and be receptive to what may need to change.

> Here is a personal example I faced on the job that may help put this principle in today's context. Since I am in sales, there is always the daunting task of ongoing prospecting. The fact is that prospecting has to be done on a regular basis. If not, there will be seasons where the pipeline of prospects will be lean. This is fairly straightforward cause and effect.
>
> A quarter end review with my manager was coming, and I knew full well I had not prospected exceptionally well the previous quarter. As a result, I had fewer opportunities in my pipeline. I knew this was going to be brought up for discussion.
>
> Instead of waiting for my manager to bring up the subject and talk to me about something I already knew, I decided

> to take a proactive approach. I knew I wanted to go to God about my job. I first admitted to Him that prospecting was an area in which I needed His help to do better. When the time came for the meeting, I took the initiative and brought up the subject with confidence. I addressed it head-on. I took full ownership of the fact that the pipeline was lean.
>
> I could approach the situation with more mental clarity because I understood that ultimately I was working for God's approval and not for my manager's. I wanted to make adjustments in prospecting because they would help me honor God in my work.
>
> At the end of my review meeting, not only did I feel good, I know my manager felt positive as well. Instead of feeling stress and anxiety over the looming issue, I felt empowered and capable. Admitting first to God where I needed to improve and then being willing to talk with my manager about these areas was key. I know God was ultimately honored in the whole process.

Randy's story gives hope that constructive criticism can be well received if our hearts are clear and we're certain of our ultimate worth through relationship with God. Randy goes on to show how good, clear, healthy communication that affirms one's self and the other person can be a catalyst for growing and strengthening relationships in community:

> I also recognized I needed to constructively handle responses to areas that I felt were not valid criticisms. Many times there were real reasons why something was not done on time, and it was equally important for me to state the facts in a professional manner. I found several factors to be important: 1) I needed to take ownership for the situation, 2) I needed to demonstrate that I understood exactly what was being said, 3) I needed to agree with valid points, and 4) I needed to see I was fully understood as well.
>
> Making changes in our lives and adjusting is hard. We love our comfort zones. Yet God is continually shaping and

> molding each of us into the likeness of Christ. This requires adopting an attitude of surrender and a lifestyle of being open to change.

How we interpret critique and criticism makes a big difference in how we respond. If we believe critique or criticism signals failure, we need to assess what failure ultimately means. Does it mean we are worthless? Or does it mean we now have an opportunity to improve something, that it's a challenge to better living? We may look at critique or criticism as a signal that someone else thinks enough of us to help us grow. If that's the case, we have a chance to strengthen the threads of community. Perspective and perception play a powerful part in how we hear and process this inevitable experience of life.

Sometimes the critique brings an opportunity to practice our straight-shooter skills (see chapter 5). Mary says, "I resolved recently to not make excuses for anything that goes wrong on the job or at home. I am practicing simple apologies instead."

Receiving Instruction

"Refuse good advice and watch your plans fail; take good counsel and watch them succeed...Listen to good advice if you want to live well, an honored guest among wise men and women" (Proverbs 15:22,31 MSG). What a relief it can be to move out of our self-protective, know-it-all bubbles and plug in to the best of the collective wisdom of those who have gone before us and those who are seeking to be wise now. I confess that I often don't want to seek the instruction of others because I don't want to appear like I don't have it all together. The paradox is that I end up looking more like a fool. Listening to and accepting good advice is like relaxing into the sturdy threads of a well-built hammock. We can breathe more fully and deeply. We can enjoy the benefits described by yet another proverb: "Take good counsel and accept correction—that's the way to live wisely and well" (19:20 MSG). At the end of the day that's certainly what I want—to live wisely and well!

Careful listening to wise instruction brings special benefits to our lives. These include:

- *Successful plans*—"For lack of guidance a nation falls, but many advisers make victory sure" (Proverbs 11:14).
- *Robust life and whole-body health*—"Dear friend, listen well to my words; tune your ears to my voice. Keep my message in plain view at all times. Concentrate! Learn it by heart! Those who discover these words live, really live; body and soul, they're bursting with health" (Proverbs 4:20-22 MSG).
- *Staying out of trouble*—"Dear friend, pay close attention to this, my wisdom; listen very closely to the way I see it. Then you'll acquire a taste for good sense; what I tell you will keep you out of trouble" (Proverbs 5:1-2 MSG).
- *Recognizing and keeping good company*—"So, friends, listen to me, take these words of mine most seriously. Don't fool around with a woman like that; don't even stroll through her neighborhood. Countless victims come under her spell; she's the death of many a poor man. She runs a halfway house to hell, fits you out with a shroud and a coffin" (Proverbs 7:24-27 MSG).
- *Happiness of the best quality*—"So, my dear friends, listen carefully; those who embrace these my ways are most blessed. Mark a life of discipline and live wisely; don't squander your precious life. Blessed the man, blessed the woman, who listens to me, awake and ready for me each morning, alert and responsive as I start my day's work. When you find me, you find life, real life, to say nothing of God's good pleasure" (Proverbs 8:32-35 MSG).
- *Recognition as a wise person*—"Intelligent children listen to their parents; foolish children do their own thing. The good acquire a taste for helpful conversation; bullies

> push and shove their way through life" (Proverbs 13:1-2 MSG).

The more we listen to and apply the guidance of wise counsel, the deeper and firmer our relationship grows with Lady Wisdom, as personified in the book of Proverbs.

When receiving feedback or instruction, we'll have the best success and experience if we approach the interaction from a place of strength rather than a place of guardedness and defensiveness. Here are a few tips that will enable us to graciously and wisely get the most from feedback or instruction:

- *Take responsibility.* Know your own thoughts, opinions, and feelings on the subject you're getting feedback or instruction about. You're not controlled by external forces or the opinion of others. Weigh what you hear with care and discernment.
- *Focus on what is accurate and helpful.* If we focus on trying to catch our conversation partner in inaccuracies or key in on what isn't helpful to us, we can throw the whole intent of the conversation off or confuse the issue.
- *Don't contradict.* Whatever your critic or instructor is saying is important to him or her. Remember that he or she is entering the conversation with a different perspective or frame of reference than you are. If you want to voice a disagreement, wait until the person is done and then say, "Yes, and..." instead of "Yes, but..."
- *Summarize regularly.* Take a few moments every so often to go over what you and your conversation partner have said and where you are in the discussion up to that point.
- *Avoid accusations, criticisms, negative innuendos, blaming, complaining, and clamming up.* Each of these

signals we are frightened, angry, and defensive. This won't benefit the exchange.

We'll have the healthiest relationships with ourselves and with others when we weigh critique and instruction with an open mind and an open heart. But we don't have to completely swallow critique or completely disregard it. Dr. Perle Thompson observes, "There are two kinds of failures: the man who will do nothing he is told, and the man who will do nothing else." Employing a spirit of self-understanding, careful listening, wisdom, and graciousness will help you decide what to do with critique and instruction.

❧ "Can I Take It?" Sound Check ❧

Receiving critique or negative feedback can be tough, but there are some ways to approach the situation that can make it more productive and positive. Respond to the following questions using this scale:

5=ALWAYS 4=OFTEN 3=SOMETIMES 2=RARELY 1=NEVER

____ 1. I receive critique and instruction with discernment and appropriate openness.

____ 2. In receiving critique and instruction, I remember that my worth is ultimately in being a child of God.

____ 3. I receive critique and instruction without seeing it as a signal of failure.

____ 4. I receive critique and instruction with humility and wisdom, carefully listening to wise counsel and wise counselors.

____ 5. When I receive critique or instruction, I take responsibility for what I believe needs to change in myself.

If your score is closer to 25, you probably know how to receive critique and feedback with grace and without feeling threatened. You take what others have to say and use what you can to make yourself a better person. If your score is lower, concentrate on how you can use the principles in this chapter to become more comfortable receiving critique and instruction. What do you need to understand more deeply your worth? How can wise instruction from wise counselors help you handle constructive criticism?

MORSELS TO CHEW ON

1. In which interaction are you most likely to encounter criticism and critique? What is the basic nature of the relationship between you and the other person?

2. The last time you experienced a positive interaction when being critiqued, what were the dynamics? How was it presented? How did you respond?

3. The last time you experienced a negative interaction when being critiqued, what were the dynamics? How was it presented? How did you respond?

4. What can we learn from King David's response to the prophet Nathan?

5. What is your definition of failure? Of success? Are there any adjustments you can make to facilitate better reception of critique and instruction?

6. Of the list of reasons from the book of Proverbs to listen to good instruction, which ones appeal the most to you? When have you experienced the benefits of listening to good instruction?

7. Which of the tips for getting the most out of feedback are strong points for you? Which need some attention?

Dear God, thank you for the wise and loving people in my life who offer feedback and instruction. Help me to graciously receive what they have to offer. Enable me to know what I need to keep and what to downplay. Even if it isn't presented well, help me make the most of the essence of the truth you want me to hear. Keep my mind wise and my heart open to learn all I can.

In Christ's name, amen.

A clay pot sitting in the sun will always be a clay pot. It has to go through the white heat of the furnace to become porcelain.

Mildred W. Struven

10

Threads of Forgiveness

Forgiveness is the answer to the child's dream of a miracle by which what is broken is made whole again, what is soiled is again made clean.

Dag Hammerskjold

Oftentimes as we work through receiving criticism or instruction and offering criticism or instruction we find the need to strengthen the fabric of our communities with threads of forgiveness. These threads are deeply transformational because they are echoes of the foundation of our life with our Creator—restoration of relationships by confessing where the blocks to communion and communication are. Forgiveness threads restore trust, expand our awareness of the wonder and gentleness of life, help us clarify what we want and hope for in ourselves and our relationships, and repair the damage done when we've been immature or disrespectful in our dealings with others.

Cultivating a smart mouth means extending forgiveness as well as asking for forgiveness.

The Art of Forgiving

If there was ever a passage of Scripture that summed up what happens when we're angry and not wanting to forgive, it's Ephesians 4:31-32 NASB: "Let all bitterness and wrath and anger and clamor and slander be put away from you, along with all malice. Be kind to one another, tender-hearted, forgiving each another, just as God in Christ also has forgiven you." The words used to describe our state of mind, even a much-hidden state of mind, are jarring and help us understand why it's so important to articulate forgiveness. Bitterness, wrath, anger, and clamor are certain to eat away at our physical bodies, just as they undermine and rot the foundations of relationships.

> Of the Seven Deadly Sins, anger is possibly the most fun. To lick your wounds, to smack your lips over grievances long past, to roll over your tongue the prospect of bitter confrontations still to come, to savor to the last toothsome morsel both the pain you are given and the pain you are giving back—in many ways it is a feast fit for a king. The chief drawback is that what you are wolfing down is yourself. The skeleton at the feast is you.[1]

Fascinating studies that have no particular spiritual base but still illuminate the human condition are now being done at universities. Scientists and sociologists are finding that unforgiveness is not good for us, and forgiveness is.

Two words in the Ephesians passage give us clues as to why forgiveness may be hard for us: "kind" and "tenderhearted." Our culture tends to value abrasiveness and tough-heartedness. Softies get squashed. Gentleness is for losers. Vulnerability is for wimps. But as Christians we are to be countercultural, and that's sometimes a scary proposition. Part of our problem is that we've forgotten what a powerhouse kindness truly is. Rabbi Abraham Joshua Heschel is reported to have said near the end of his life, "When I was young, I used to admire intelligent people; as I grow older, I admire kind people."[2]

Even though it may be counterintuitive, extending forgiveness is really for the hearty, the strong, the bold, and the persistent. It's a process that takes a while to work through. And it's an intentional choice that sometimes must be made day after day until it's solidly woven into the fabric of your being. It takes persistence, fortitude, and strength to stay with the process.

❧ "Forgiveness" Sound Check ❧

Being able to give and receive forgiveness is truly a distinguishing mark of someone with a smart mouth. Respond to each statement with the following scale:

5=ALWAYS 4=OFTEN 3=SOMETIMES 2=RARELY 1=NEVER

____ 1. When I forgive someone, I'm willing to go the extra step and tell them I don't want them to behave in that way anymore.

____ 2. I can tell someone I forgive them—and act on it—even if my heart doesn't yet...because I know God has.

____ 3. I forgive others because I know there's always more to the story than meets the eye.

____ 4. I know that even after some things are forgiven, additional effort might be needed for complete healing and resolution.

____ 5. When I've done something I need forgiveness for, I go directly and discretely to the person involved and seek forgiveness.

The Forgiveness Sound Check has a scale of 5 to 25, with scores closer to 25 indicating forgiveness is something you practice for yourself and others. You're probably comfortable giving and receiving grace. If your score is lower, where do you need to be more forgiving of yourself and others? How can you better understand and experience the forgiveness of God more fully?

Clemency Not Tolerance

Telling people they are forgiven is not the same as saying something is OK. Pastor Tom Walker of Palms Presbyterian Church in Florida taught his sons that they don't tell each other "It's OK" if one has to apologize to the other for a physical, mental, or emotional transgression. Hitting is not OK. Instead they are to say, "I forgive you." There's a world of difference! Each of us has experienced hurts that aren't OK. We still need to forgive because it sets in motion potent and mysterious reweavings of our community fabric. But we don't need to negate what we experienced or pretend it never happened. You can see how forgiveness isn't for the faint of heart.

Depending on the nature of your relationship with the person who has wronged you, there is a significant phrase you can use that might deepen your relationship and solidify the forgiveness in ways that are truly close to the heart of God. Jesus is our model:

> Jesus went to the Mount of Olives. At dawn he appeared again in the temple courts, where all the people gathered around him, and he sat down to teach them. The teachers of the law and the Pharisees brought in a woman caught in adultery. They made her stand before the group and said to Jesus, "Teacher, this woman was caught in the act of adultery. In the Law Moses commanded us to stone such women. Now what do you say?" They were using this question as a trap, in order to have a basis for accusing him.
>
> But Jesus bent down and started to write on the ground with his finger. When they kept on questioning him, he straightened up and said to them, "If any one of you is without sin, let him be the first to throw a stone at her." Again he stooped down and wrote on the ground.
>
> At this, those who heard began to go away one at a time, the older ones first, until only Jesus was left, with the woman still standing there. Jesus straightened up and asked her, "Woman, where are they? Has no one condemned you?"
>
> "No one, sir," she said.
>
> "Then *neither do I condemn you,*" Jesus declared. "Go now and *leave your life of sin*" (John 8:1-11).

"I forgive you" takes you and the other person to a deep and sacred space in your relationship. To take the relationship even further, to ensure the person that you expect communication and companionship to continue, you can use your smart mouth to say, "And please don't do it again." Jesus knew that the woman's behavior drove a wedge between her and God. Jesus wanted her to stop the behavior so the relationship could deepen and she could become the woman of magnificence she was created to be. We can show the same kind of loving confidence in someone when we indicate to him or her that we see better in his or her character than what has been forgiven.

Going even deeper into the heart of God, we also need to realize that even if we can't say to someone with integrity, "I forgive you," we can say, "You are forgiven" because they are, and we just have to work at catching up with God's reality. We aren't allowed to hold someone else hostage for something already forgiven. And, in fact, not forgiving the person is really holding ourselves hostage!

One of the most compelling reasons forgiveness requires strength is we must shed the puniness of our own limited perspective and find the freedom and mind-bending joy of seeing things from another's perspective. As we saw in chapter 1, none of us ever really knows the whole story behind the actions of others. The smart mouth voices forgiveness anyway.

My dear friend Cheri shared this powerful story with me.

> My family was pretty much the poster family for dysfunction. I guess you could say we put the fun in dysfunction. Oh, our parents loved us, but both of my parents grew up in families that needed a good dose of God's wisdom and love. They didn't get the actual truths on how He loves everyone, no matter where they are in life, and there's no guilt attached to poor decisions. So when I was growing up guilt pervaded our home. Guilt in feelings of failing as a parent, guilt passed on to every child (all seven of us) stemming from parents who simply didn't know how to love unconditionally.
>
> I guess I didn't fully realize the lack of unconditional love and affection until I married the world's greatest man, who had unconditional love for me. Wow, was that weird! If I messed up, he still

said he loved me and it was okay! How strange. Then, when we had our two beautiful girls, I realized there was something deep in me that had been missing for a long time, maybe even forever. I looked at these two precious children and felt overwhelmed by a love I had never felt. It was as if God showed me how He loved me (I didn't know that at the time because I didn't know Him yet). We loved these children and that love could *never* go away. It could never be taken away by any act they did. I got it...unconditional love!

Then came anger. Anger against my parents who never gave me that. Many years passed—in fact 16—of simply not understanding how parents could not act like they loved their kids (I need to say I was *completely* wrong, but I'll get to that soon). My husband and I became Christians almost 11 years ago, so I knew God didn't want me harboring these feelings. But there was a place inside me that made excuses on why I couldn't forgive. You know, things like thinking I had "righteous anger," and that God was probably mad at them too. Good grief, I did...and still have...so much to learn about Him. I didn't get it until our family was *thumped* on the head—hard, I might add.

Two years ago my mom's husband was diagnosed with liver and colon cancer. Talk about a breathtaking moment. It was as if I suddenly saw her for what she truly was...a woman who did love. A woman who was getting her heart ripped out by a terrible disease. A woman who had no control over anything. I saw her vulnerability, her courage, her compassion for him, and it made me stop in my tracks. I know God was all over her and my emotions because my old self would've questioned her and been mad that I never got that love. Instead God showed me how to give her grace. I instantly felt as if I needed to take care of her, needed to be there for her no matter what.

I'd never experienced these feelings about her before. In fact, I told my brothers and sisters how sad it was going to be to see her a lonely old lady since she had turned away her kids. I wasn't angry; I just felt sad for her. I questioned God about what good could come out of this, you know, from the Scriptures that say we aren't given things we can't handle and how He doesn't leave us...I just didn't understand how He could allow this. I still am amazed how selfish I was/am.

I *know* in my very soul that those Scriptures are true. How dare the enemy try to make me waver on that. I know God is full of grace and love, and He is constantly calling on us to draw closer to Him. I know this because over the year that my stepdad was sick, watching his body be destroyed by cancer, my mom, in my eyes, was growing into the woman I always wanted her to be. Needless to say, she had always been like that, I just didn't realize it. My heart was being strangled by unforgiveness.

It wasn't until the very end of his life that Mom and I had a chance to talk, really talk, about what it was like for her as a mom, dealing with things I had no idea she was dealing with. I realized that she wasn't giving conditional love and she wasn't being selfish. She was protecting her children from abuse. She had taken on the burden of an abusive husband (not my stepdad) without me even knowing it! As she told me these things, I sat in awe. The woman whom I was so angry at, whom I only talked to maybe once a month, the woman whom I thought was so selfish, was now humbly telling me all that she went through *and* admitting she wasn't the perfect wife either.

In my overwhelming desire to say "Shut up!" (in a "no way" kind of tone), I was simply struck by how God used this terrible disease, this terrible circumstance, to show our family how much He's been there for us and how much He loves us.

Right before my stepdad died, all my siblings and I wrote him letters. I thanked him for taking care of Mom, for making her happy. I felt I needed to tell him we would take care of her, that we loved her more than ever, and she would not be lonely. So I did just that. I spelled it all out for him...and her...because his eyes weren't working as well as they used to. I wasn't there, but I can picture her reading this letter to him, hearing how I loved her and that her children would be taking care of her, wanting to build a relationship with her. My letter told him that I know God used this terrible thing that was happening to him in a way that would glorify Him.

How good is God? My breath still catches in my throat when I think about it. I am happy to report that I talk to my mom daily. She is a wonderful mother and grandmother. I love my mom unconditionally, and I know she loves me the same way. She has the same

> desires and feelings I do: love, happiness, sadness, the desire to feel loved. Not only can I say I love her, but for once in my life I can truly say I forgive her. For that, God gets all of the glory.
>
> I know this note is long. Robin, maybe someday you'll be talking to someone who might be going through a similar situation. You'll have the chance to share God's amazing redemption and grace in my family members' lives.

And here's where I sound like one of those funny infomercials: "But wait, there's more!" When I called Cheri to ask her if it was really okay to print this very personal, very powerful story, she said, "Oh yes! I've shared it with the whole family, and it changed the way we interact. We all have a much better picture of what our family is all about. And my mom would be happy for this to be printed."

Cheri's full story illustrates the impact of getting things out in the open, of trying to see things and people as clearly as possible, of using the smart mouth of forgiveness to reweave the threads of family and redeem, restore, and reenergize relationships. That seems to be God's specialty as we use the potent tools he has given us to assist in bringing about his hopes and dreams for the world.

Finally, forgiveness takes strength because there will most certainly be issues that are not forgotten and still need healing. Isn't it great how God is constantly refining us, helping us forgive and love the people around us?

It Might Set Off a Reaction

One of my dear and longtime friends shared a story with me that illustrates the positive chain that asking for and receiving forgiveness can start. Threads of community can be repaired and a stronger, more resilient pattern emerges.

> The other day my sister came over for lunch. We "do lunch" as often as we can, but this time was different. There were just four of us: my sister, me, and our two little girls. We were all sitting on the family room floor, and my sister said she had something to share with me.

"I don't want to get all emotional or anything, but there is something that has been on my mind for a very long time that I have wanted to talk to you about." She then told me she had recently gone to Bible study at her church and the leader said repeatedly, "Never use the Bible as a weapon." My sister went on to tell me how sorry she was for being involved in an incident seven years earlier that had hurt me very much.

She and another family member had not approved of a situation I had chosen to be in. One evening she and the other family member asked me to come to her apartment. The other family member read Scripture to me and told me he and God didn't approve of my choices. The approach was condemning and not very loving. My sister expressed concern over the choice I was making. I eventually left my sister's apartment and could not believe what had just transpired. I was so hurt by the words and tone the other family member had used, and I was hurt that my sister was sitting there being involved in it.

I wrote them letters expressing how hurt I was, but we didn't talk about it again. In my heart I had already forgiven them. I didn't want this incident to ruin our relationship.

But now, seven years later, my sister told me how sorry she was for being involved in that situation. She didn't approve of the way the other family member handled it; she didn't feel it was a very loving approach. She repeated what her Bible-study leader had said and expressed that it had struck her and made her think of that evening.

I was surprised. I didn't know she even remembered it. She asked for my forgiveness. I told her I forgave her, that I had forgiven her a long time ago.

But the conversation sparked something in me. There was something in my heart I had been carrying a long time, something I wanted to share with her. I apologized for going out on a date with a man she'd wanted to go out with. I didn't realize it would bother her or me to go out with him because my sister was dating the man she eventually married. But at the time, when I told her I had gone out with this man, I could tell she was hurt. I felt terrible about it but never admitted it. I asked her forgiveness, and she forgave me.

My sister and I have definitely had our ups and downs throughout the years, but this moment was wonderful. It was very healing and brought us closer together not only as sisters but also as friends.

The Art of Receiving Forgiveness

"Fools mock at making amends for sin, but goodwill is found among the upright" (Proverbs 14:9). We will never truly have smart mouths or smart anything else if we don't take seriously our need to ask for forgiveness.

A smart mouth understands the power of confession, as well as what constitutes appropriate confession.

"He who conceals his sins does not prosper, but whoever confesses and renounces them finds mercy" (Proverbs 28:13). When you have done something that needs confessing, go directly to the person whom your transgression offended. Make peace; accept forgiveness.

One of my favorite images of confession is "run to the roar." The expression comes from the idea that when a group of lions is stalking prey, they designate one lion to stand up and roar, hopefully scaring the prey into running into the circle of lions hidden in waiting. If the prey runs to the roar, they are less likely to be ensnared by the hunters. Although not necessarily factual, this is a good picture of dealing with sin. Don't wait for your sin to come looking for you. When you know you need to confess, go and do it quickly and appropriately.

Appropriate means you involve only the parties who really need to know. You give a truthful accounting of the wrong and make an apology for the consequences. Next you offer to make things right and turn from the transgression in the future. To give up the sin frees you from guilt and helps you not repeat the practice in the future.

Some of us have a quirky compulsion to confess over and over to as many people as will listen. Someone with a smart mouth understands that once something is confessed and (hopefully) forgiven (it most certainly is by God), we can move on and continue to commune with God without having to talk about the transgression again. If you tend to confess again and again, talk to a trusted spiritual advisor who can help you move from guilt and shame to grace and confidence.

Granting and seeking forgiveness is always a decision. Pursuing it may seem irrational at times, but it is always the right choice to make. Deciding to forgive brings you power and joy. Deciding to be forgiven brings you peace and the great energy that comes from being set free. Deciding to forgive also keeps you from being lonely. "Overlook an offense and bond a friendship; fasten on to a slight and—good-bye friend!" (Proverbs 17:9 MSG).

When we engage in forgiveness from either side of the fence, we allow the transformation of our minds as we view things and people from a fresh, more open-hearted perspective. By speaking words of forgiveness and confession, we unlock our hearts and minds to more deeply understand the mystery of God's amazing, unconditional love for us.

Morsels to Chew On

1. Think about a time when you were forgiven. What was the experience like?

2. Is it important that you understand the forgiveness of God before you try to forgive yourself or someone else? Why or why not?

3. Can you forgive someone and still tell that person what he or she did is not OK?

4. What kind of relationship did Jesus set up with the woman caught in adultery when he didn't condemn her and said, "Go now and leave your life of sin"? Who in your life might need to hear that from you?

5. What spiritual reality do you affirm when you tell someone "You are forgiven" even if you don't want to say "I forgive you"?

6. Knowing more about a situation or the background for someone's attitudes and behaviors helps you be more forgiving. Is there someone you're having trouble forgiving? Is there some way you could approach this person to find out more? Are you willing to forgive even if you don't get the whole story?

7. Why is forgiveness wise?

8. Is there something you need to confess and receive forgiveness for? How might this strengthen the fabric of your community? What does it mean to you to "run to the roar"?

Loving and forgiving God, by understanding the model of your grace, mercy, and love of reconciliation, I have a road map for what it means to forgive. I realize I don't always want to follow that map, so I ask for the willingness to get closer to you so I have the strength to forgive. It takes persistence and grit to forgive. It takes tenderness of heart and mind. This is a hard thing to do!

Lord, give me the grace and strength of spirit I need to make confession, ask for and receive forgiveness from you, from myself, and from others. I want my relationships to be a true reflection of you.

Help me be wise and loving in this area of my life.

In Christ's name, amen.

Forgiveness is man's deepest need and highest achievement.

HORACE BUSHNELL

11

Thanks, I Needed That!

The highest wisdom is kindness.

The Talmud

One kind word can warm three winter months.

Japanese proverb

In our adventure in partnering with God to be people who strengthen the fabric of relationship and community, encouragement is one of the most pleasant and simplest tools to use. When we use our words to encourage, we are helping others "live in courage." We need to do this all the time for everyone. Receiving encouragement is a basic human necessity in a spiritual, mental, and emotional sense. People thrive on it. Encouragement is one of the lubricants of human functioning.

There are seven primary ways we can encourage each other. If we build these into our days, our mouths will indeed be very smart and uplifting!

"I Bless You"

Throughout the Old Testament the giving of a formal blessing was the difference between life and death. The blessing meant your parents believed in you, your community believed in you, and ultimately you recognized that God believed in you. It also meant that anyone who messed with you would find themselves in a pickle with many people to answer to.

Today we can receive blessings on a regular basis. The benediction in your weekly worship service is not meant to be the signal to pick up your belongings, put on your coat, and leave. This potent part of the service should be carefully listened to, savored, written down, and recalled throughout the coming week. In offering the benediction, your minister is speaking blessing over you to encourage your faith, to enliven your spirit, to enfold you in the days ahead with the recognition of God's presence.

As you look at the opening and closing of many of the apostle Paul's letters to the churches he nurtured, you'll see that the words he uses are not just nice Christian words that are sanctified ways of saying hello and goodbye. His words are living, moving, and exciting calls to Christians to pay attention to the best, highest, and most powerful reality moving in their midst. He knew that if the Corinthians took seriously his opening blessing of "grace and peace to you from God our Father and the Lord Jesus Christ," they would be a tremendous people making a powerhouse impact in their community (2 Corinthians 1:2). As he finishes a prayer for his Ephesians friends, Paul says, "Now to him who is able to do immeasurably more than all we ask or imagine, according to his power that is at work within us, to him be glory in the church and in Christ Jesus throughout all generations, for ever and ever! Amen" (3:20-21). Do you know what could happen in your life if you truly believed and lived this? Do you know what could happen in the lives of others if you offered them blessings like this?

When we take this reality seriously, we can see how a heartfelt blessing can be one of the greatest gifts to give and a potentially life-changing gift to receive.

"I Believe in You"

Telling people you believe in them is "the right word at the right time—beautiful" (Proverbs 15:23 MSG). Such a gift to give! Such a treasure to receive! When we falter in our belief in ourselves, we're encouraged that others believe in us. They could be teachers, friends, family members, and employers. Their belief in us, and in God in us, encourages us to continue with what we believe we are meant to be and do. When we feel unworthy, the encouragement of someone helps restore our courage by letting us know we are worthy of support, esteem, and assurance.

You can also be blessed by the encouragement of an offspring. One mom shared this when I asked for input on a moment of encouragement:

> During the late-1980s I was in the midst of preparing for my second career. More than 50 years of age, I didn't want to remain an elementary teacher past the point when I felt my ability to banter and build rapport with sixth-graders was sustainable. Therefore I was pursuing a masters degree in social work and hoped to fulfill a lifelong desire by becoming a licensed clinical social worker.
>
> One day while sitting on the front porch of my blue colonial Virginia home, for a moment I faced a bit of reality. By the time I could begin work as a therapist, I would be "old." I said to my young-adult daughter, "By the time I get my degree and get licensed, I will be in my rocking chair. Should I even be pursuing this dream?"
>
> My daughter said to me, "And how old do you think you will be if you don't do it?"
>
> I laughed. I still laugh about that moment. Eventually I retired from teaching, became licensed, and had the time of my life in my second career.

My own kids have been encouraging to me in sometimes humorous ways. As I was getting nearer and nearer to my submission deadline for this book, I must have started showing signs of mild distress (this happens to writers a lot). One day while driving in the car with then 11-year-old Grant, I let out a big, long, full sigh.

Grant said, "Mom! Why such a huge sigh?"

I answered, "Oh, I don't know, honey. I guess I'm a little worried that the book won't meet its word quota when it's time to turn it in."

You know, you should always be very careful of the kind of counsel you give your children when *they* are in distress. It will always come back to you. Grant said, "Well, Mom, whenever I'm stressed about a project you tell me to just stop worrying and get to work!"

I didn't know whether to laugh or cry. But I did say, "Honey, would you repeat that one more time?" I wanted both of us to hear it again for present and future reference. He did and I stopped sighing.

Expecting the best for and out of people is another expression of believing in them. What if for a week or so you said "Good morning" or "Good night" to people and really meant it? What if you used the power of your words to speak the blessing of goodness over their time in an intentional and heartfelt way? Those genuine words might take root in their lives. Maybe you'd soon really want to know if they had a good morning or a good night. By giving deliberate blessing, a blessing you actually think about instead of just being a nice formality, you increase your awareness of the people around you. They might notice that you actually want them to have a good morning, a good day, or a good night. And that's a great thing!

We encourage others by believing the best in them as we gently point out, maybe not even directly, that we expect and hope better for them and from them than they are willing to recognize right then. We encourage others to be better versions of themselves when we speak positively instead of complaining. My friend Cheree observes, "The hardest thing to tame about my mouth is the urge to jump on the bandwagon when I'm in the midst of complainers. God has blessed me with so much, so why do I want to fit in by finding fault with things? Too often women get in a little contest of who has the worst luck. It's important to walk away from those conversations rather than take part." Whether you actively speak up and counter the negativity or quietly remove yourself from the complaining, you let people know you believe better of them than what they're engaged in at that moment.

❧ "Encouragement" Sound Check ❧

One of the best tasks we have as we communicate with others is to encourage. Use the following scale in responding to each statement:

5=ALWAYS 4=OFTEN 3=SOMETIMES 2=RARELY 1=NEVER

____ 1. I bless others, imparting grace and goodness into their lives.

____ 2. I tell others I believe in them and I expect the best for them and from them because they are unique children of God and members of God's community.

____ 3. I tell others I love them.

____ 4. I express appreciation for others by telling them thank you out loud, in writing, and nonverbally through acts of gratitude or touch.

____ 5. I let people know when I've been prompted to think about them.

____ 6. I celebrate with people by letting them know I'm happy for them when good things happen in their lives.

____ 7. I make a specific effort to let people know I'm supporting them when sad things happen in their lives.

____ 8. I'm a publicist for others, letting them know I value them as I tell other people about their good character or deeds.

When you score closer to 40 on this scale, you are very good at encouraging others, and it probably shows in your relationships. If your score is lower, how can you improve in each of the statements? Choose one area to improve in each week, noting specific actions you can take. Become an encourager of others!

"I Love You"

"Pleasant words are a honeycomb, sweet to the soul and healing to the bones" (Proverbs 16:24). Sometimes the encouragement of love comes right out of the blue. My teenaged daughter sent me a text message late one evening that I picked up the following morning. What prompted her to send the message, I don't really know. But when I clicked on the message screen, it simply said, "I love you mommy." No reason included; no request for funds attached. Simple, pure, and spontaneous love. I became completely refreshed, awash in the understanding that regardless of the kind of mommy I feel I am, I am loved and those around me feel loved by me.

"I Appreciate You"

Expressing appreciation is a highly encouraging way for us to speak to others. Do this often and watch your world transform into "the kingdom come on earth as it is in heaven." In this sometimes harsh and negative world, people need to know they're valued and thought about in a positive way. Words of appreciation sometimes catch people off guard because of the way we're conditioned by everyday circumstances. My friend Carolyn likes to "ambush" people with appreciation:

> I once worked for a boss who taught me a very good lesson. Even more important than complaining about bad service is complimenting someone on good service. He always made sure to seek out the manager and let them know about a good experience. Since then I've always tried to do that, and it's great fun! You should see the look on managers' faces when they get called over to receive praise instead of a complaint! They're braced for the worst and get something completely unexpected. It makes both of our days.
>
> And it's even more fun to find out that the person who gave the good service was rewarded somehow for it. My all-time favorite was writing a letter to compliment our real estate agent. In purchasing our first home, he gave us some great financial advice that saved us several thousand dollars. I wrote to his manager to praise the agent and thank them for giving such great service to their customers. A few weeks later I was

> thrilled to receive a thank-you note from our agent describing how the manager had read my letter during a district-wide meeting. The manager had left our agent's name until the very end so he could call our agent up as everyone applauded. That still makes me happy 13 years later. He'll always remember that!

I love Heather's candor when she says, "As a mother I know how much I do for other people. It's a needed affirmation to hear 'please' and 'thank you'—especially on laundry days when I'm up and down a hundred times. Hearing 'please' and 'thank you' motivates me to get back up to get that cup of milk when my seat didn't even have time to get warm yet." We all want to experience appreciation, and a true trick to relationships is finding out what constitutes meaningful appreciation to someone and then supplying it!

One day just before Mother's Day a few years ago, I had the honor of speaking with a group of third graders about writing and publishing books. One little guy I'll call Brendon was particularly engaging and lively. He had lots of energy and lots to say. No grass was going to grow under Brendon, that was certain.

While talking about books I handed each of them one of my books on mothering and tried to weave a little Mother's Day message into my technical talk about writing. I wanted to steer them to thinking of gifts they could give their moms that wouldn't cost them any money. I introduced them to the chapter on gratitude and asked what they thought two of a mom's favorite words were to hear.

Brendon perked right up and said, "Good night?" The adults in the room howled with laughter as we had all "been there, done that" about getting our kids to bed for some peace and quiet.

As we refocused on the topic of gratitude, the kids began to understand that "thank you" can be a powerful gift to their moms. Appreciation, recognition, gratitude—all can be just the nudge people need to keep going when they feel like they're about to run out of fuel.

I've had several instances when the pleasant words of appreciation from my son, Grant, have definitely been sweet to my soul. He seems to have an uncanny knack for thanking me or hugging me at just the right time in my day. He is so pleasant and polite and thoughtful and encouraging. When he says of his ham-and-cheese sandwich, "Thank you, Mommy, for this sandwich you made me," my heart is cleansed and whatever thought I was lost in evaporates as I drink in the wonderful elixir of someone appreciating what I have done.

Mothers (and dads too) do need and thrive on the encouragement of appreciation. Tell your parents words of gratitude today!

Mary reminds us that written appreciation is just as dear if not more so at times than spoken appreciation: "A precious friend writes the most wonderful thank-you notes. She has a way of letting you know of her love and appreciation in a simple, flowing style. I know if she is involved in anything I do I will receive one of her heart-warming messages. I have come to anticipate (not expect or take for granted) them because of the dear things she says. I know I'm on her mind, and it makes me feel very special." Written appreciation lets the receiver dwell on and experience it more than once!

Our appreciative encouragement can come in nonverbal forms as well. Wouldn't you like to be appreciated like this? It comes from Elizabeth, who is forever dreaming up ways to tell others how important they are.

> Last summer Jane Chilton, Amy Groves, and I surprised Gwen Paten and took her out for an "I Love Gwen" lunch. She'd been ultra swamped at work. The women's ministry leader was retiring, and Gwen was doing everything and then some. We could tell she needed to be "appreciated." We got to the restaurant before she did, bringing a beautiful bouquet of flowers. We ate outside on the patio in the bright sunshine and just doted over her. It really helped her spirit. A few *hours* later we were all recharged and ready for the world again!

In whatever way we show gratitude, it's important that it be expressed. As Gladys Stein said, "Silent gratitude isn't much use to anyone."

"I Thought About You"

"Like cold water to a weary soul is good news from a distant land" (Proverbs 25:25). Often we can be encouraged by a phone call, Email, or a note that lets us know someone far away is doing well, perhaps has recovered from surgery, has gotten a new job, or has had a prodigal child return home. Maybe the good news is simply that they thought of us with love and affection and wanted to let us know! Proverbs 25:25 says to stay in touch with people. In our society so many families live far apart, and a good word from a close-yet-distant relative can make someone's day. It's always encouraging to know someone thought of us.

"I Am Happy for You"

Celebration is the backbone of communities growing, of them being strengthened and confirmed. When we celebrate with each other, we highlight the best of what we are, what we do, and what we have. When we tell people we are happy for them, it brings a glow to their faces.

It also fortifies us as people of generous spirits. We all know it's not always easy to be happy for other people, especially if things aren't going the way we want them to in our own lives. Maybe this is why Paul suggested to his friends in Rome, "Rejoice with those who rejoice; mourn with those who mourn" (Romans 12:15). Getting out of ourselves enough to be truly empathic with others is healthy for us and encouraging to them.

Jesus knew the power of spending time with people at celebrations. He attended weddings and dinner parties. He knew when people gather together they bond in special ways.

"I Am with You"

Jesus also attended funerals. As important as it is for us to encourage others by celebrating with them, Paul also reminds us to mourn with those who mourn. Letting others know we are with them through verbal and nonverbal communication is deeply encouraging and strengthening.

In many ways nonverbals are more important in grief and transition than verbal communication. At a particularly difficult funeral for a young man who left behind three children and a stunned widow, I stood in line with a lovely young woman who confessed, "I don't know what to say." Having been in pastoral ministry, I assured her that our friend was in such a condition that she really didn't hear the words we said but keenly felt our presence and our hugs. When people are grieving, scared, and exhausted, they need to have genuine people around them offering authentic support and the necessary space and time to mourn, heal, and recover. There are times when words are elusive, but a heartfelt hug or pat on the hand says what the most carefully crafted phrases cannot.

The beauty of encouraging presence is keenly felt by anyone who has ever taken comfort in the words Jesus spoke so long ago that still ring true because of the presence of his Holy Spirit: "And surely I am with you always, to the very end of the age" (Matthew 28:20). In the interest of making promises we can keep (chapter 2), we may not be able to tell someone we will be with them always, but we can offer our encouraging presence, love, and prayer now to the best of our abilities. Letting someone know he or she is remembered can be very encouraging.

"I Value You"

"Let another praise you, and not your own mouth; someone else, and not your own lips" (Proverbs 27:2). We are very encouraging to others when we compliment them to their faces, within earshot of them, or behind their backs and they hear about it later. Les and Leslie Parrott, in their meditations on Proverbs for couples, call this "being your partner's publicist."[1] I've had the joy of knowing what they're talking about. One evening when I was out to dinner with my husband and two gentlemen he was entertaining for work, my husband gave a terrific description of my work and ministry and what I was doing in its development. It was one of those moments when I fell in love with him all over again. He was proud of me, and he enjoyed what I was doing. And he was willing to lift me up in public! What a gift!

You can be a publicist for others. Don't give false flattery, for the book of Proverbs speaks of the insincerity of the flatterer. Do give enthusiastic and heartfelt praise in front of others that uplifts and honors the one you're praising. When you do it as a surprise, so much the better. Let your children overhear you singing their accolades when you're talking with someone on the phone. Praise a friend in public. Give a colleague a big verbal pat on the back in front of others. Be a walking advertisement for people you love, respect, admire, and appreciate.

One of the most moving examples of this I ever witnessed was at the welcome home rally for the Indianapolis Colts after their 2007 Super Bowl win. At that point in the season, the entire nation had become aware of the grace, faith, and humility of head coach Tony Dungy. Coach Dungy had shown himself to be a steady man of solid character.

In his thank-you speech to the fans, he looked back over his shoulder at his team and said, "Each one of these young men is someone you would be proud to call your son." Coach Dungy knows the joy and pain of having and losing a son, so his words were filled with extra meaning. He was a publicist for each member of his team. And no one doubted the sincerity of his recommendation. Coach's encouragement benefited each player on and off the field.

One of the smartest mouths I know belongs to Brian Shivers, director of Youth and College Ministries at Second Presbyterian Church in Indianapolis. He and his team touch hundreds of young lives directly each year. The team impacts thousands of lives by being transformational agents in the lives of young people, who then produce multiple ripples in their schools, families, work sites, and communities. Brian sums up the wisdom of encouragement and its power to strengthen relational threads:

> I have found it incredibly important to give accurate encouragement that reflects more on who someone is not just on

> what someone has done. I use three important phrases that can be shared with anyone. I have personally witnessed the power of these simple phrases in the lives of the young people with whom I am honored to work. The phrases: "I believe in you." "I trust you." "I love you." In a culture that tends to focus on the negative, this is huge! Even if a young person has done something destructive, I can still say "I believe in you." Even if someone has let me down, I can still say "I trust you" (because this is rooted in trusting people in who they are and not in trusting they will always make the correct choice). I can always say "I love you" because this has its foundation in commitment, in covenant. This is an intentional decision. All three are. As I remind myself to say these things, I also remind myself to do them. This is also a type of self-talk. It is "living as if these things are true." And in order to actually do these things, I must also believe in me, trust me, and love who I am.

It's no wonder people trust their children's hearts, souls, and lives to him!

Lovely Spiritual Foundation

Like the other threads we're exploring in this book, encouragement has a beautiful spiritual foundation. Why do we dare encourage others? Why should we engage in the foolishness of infusing people with the courage and strength to walk through life positively in spite of what, at times, seem to be remarkable odds? Because of the ultimate reality that surrounds our lives: "Have I not commanded you? Be strong and courageous. Do not be terrified; do not be discouraged, for the LORD your God will be with you wherever you go" (Joshua 1:9). The reality that is larger than we often acknowledge or embrace is what Jesus promised: "Peace I leave with you; my peace I give you. I do not give to you as the world gives. Do not let your hearts be troubled and do not be afraid" (John 14:27). We encourage each other because it's the only reasonable thing to do when we've experienced the ultimate affirmation of Jesus' love for us.

Morsels to Chew On

1. Think of a time when you felt encouraged by someone. What was your experience of yourself? What was your experience of the other person? How did it impact your relationship?

2. Drink in this blessing from Numbers 7:24-26: "The Lord bless you and keep you; the Lord make his face shine upon you and be gracious to you; the Lord turn his face toward you and give you peace." What are the key words in that blessing to you at this point in your life and why? How will keeping this blessing in front of you change the way you move through your day?

3. How can you give the encouragement of blessing to others?

4. Is there someone in your life right now who is trying to make a decision or move forward with a plan or undertaking? How can you be sincerely encouraging to him or her?

5. Whom do you love? Do they know? How will you let them know in the next 24 hours?

6. How can being grateful to someone set off a chain reaction of gratitude?

7. Who could use an update on your life? Who would be encouraged just to know you thought about them today? Contact them!

8. What have you found to be encouraging when you need comfort or support?

9. Who needs you to be a publicist for them?

Encouraging God, thank you for such a wondrous array of ways to encourage others in my world. Help me to be so comfortable with myself and in your love that I can be more aware of who needs encouragement and what kind of encouragement they need.

I am grateful for all the people you've put in my life who encourage me. Help me strengthen the fabric of community by asking for encouragement when I need it.

I am also grateful for your Holy Spirit, who was sent specifically to comfort and encourage. I'm glad for that comfort in my own life, and I appreciate the guidance as I encourage others.

In Christ's name, amen.

Nothing is as valuable to a man as courage.

TERENCE

12

Stop Spreadin' the News

If I lose my honor, I lose myself.

William Shakespeare

A friend who worked in the corporate world told me part of their training course was to encourage workers to be careful about who might be listening. In his corporation they were taught not to talk about a sales call until after they left the customer's building. The story was told that two salespeople were on their way out and discussing a call they had just completed. One made negative comments about the president of the company on which they had just called. You guessed it—the president was in the elevator. Do you think they made the sale?

It's a scientific fact that two objects cannot occupy the same space at the same time. It seems to be a spiritual fact that two types of talk cannot use the same breath. Every breath we use to talk is either for good, for destruction, or neutral. James made this observation about the gift of breath, vocal cords, mouth, and teeth for articulation...and anything else that we need to speak:

> This is scary: You can tame a tiger, but you can't tame a tongue—it's never been done. The tongue runs wild, a wanton killer. With our tongues we bless God our Father; with the same tongues we curse the very men and women

> he made in his image. Curses and blessings out of the same mouth!
>
> My friends, this can't go on. A spring doesn't gush fresh water one day and brackish the next, does it? Apple trees don't bear strawberries, do they? Raspberry bushes don't bear apples, do they? You're not going to dip into a polluted mud hole and get a cup of clear, cool water, are you? (James 3:7-12 MSG).

I'm pretty sure I don't want my mouth compared to a polluted mud hole, but when I use the gifts that are meant to produce good communication for gossip and trashy talk, I am in grave danger of unraveling some very important threads of community.

"Just Say No" Sound Check

Gossip and trashy talk undercut our ability to communicate well, communicate with credibility, and communicate positively to change our world. Respond to the following statements using the following scale:

5=ALWAYS 4=OFTEN 3=SOMETIMES 2=RARELY 1=NEVER

____ 1. I'm aware of when I'm tempted to gossip to fit into a conversation.

____ 2. I'm aware of when I'm tempted to gossip to turn attention away from my flaws and shortcomings.

____ 3. I'm aware of when I'm tempted to gossip to show off what I know.

____ 4. I'm comfortable asking people to stop gossiping when they are around me.

____ 5. I set clear boundaries around participating in gossip, even though I may be lonely at times.

____ 6. I physically move out of conversations that turn toward gossip.

____ 7. I avoid crass or vulgar language.

In this particularly powerful area of good communication, the scale is from 7 to 35, with 35 showing you have an excellent handle on staying away from gossip and crass language. If your score is lower, what areas are you particularly vulnerable in? Do you trip up around particular people? In particular situations or environments? What can you do to make it easier to have a smart mouth in those instances? Be on the look-out and bump up that score.

Scattering Feathers...or Worse

A nineteenth-century folktale tells of a man who went about his neighborhood gossiping about and slandering the neighborhood's wise man. One day the gossip went to the wise man's house and asked for forgiveness. Intuitively the wise man discerned that the gossip had not fully realized the gravity of his activities. So the wise man said he would forgive him on two conditions: the first was that the gossip had to go home, get a feather pillow from his house, take it out into the neighborhood where he should cut it open and let the wind scatter the feathers as it would. After he had completed this assignment, the gossip should return to the wise man's house.

The request seemed strange to the gossip, but he thought he was getting off rather easy. So he quickly cut up the pillow, watched the wind scatter the feathers, and returned to the wise man's house.

"So am I now forgiven?" he asked.

"Just one other thing," the wise man said. "Go out into the neighborhood and gather up every single feather the wind has scattered."

"But that's impossible. They are strewn everywhere!"

"Precisely," the wise man answered. "You believe that you truly want to correct the damage you've done. But it is as impossible to repair the havoc you have caused with your word as it is to recover the feathers. Your words are out in the neighborhood, spreading hate, even as we speak."

Gossip is not for the wise, not for those cultivating a smart mouth.

One of the rich rewards of having a smart mouth is being at peace.

And there are plenty of proverbs to guide us in the use of our tongue to bring peace to ourselves and to those around us. In the book of Proverbs the mention of gossip is in direct contrast to the person of peace. A gossip is one who routinely destroys the possibility of grace, compassion, and peace in a situation because he or she is the wood that keeps the fires of strife burning (Proverbs 26:20) and the one who grabs a passing dog by the ears (26:17). On the other hand, the one who puts a stop to offensive talk and hurtful conversation is a person of peace and love and great wisdom (10:11-13).

Why do we gossip? Sometimes we do it just to be included. It helps us share an identity with another. This kind of gossip is meant to be benign; it is honestly not meant to hurt others. When I sit at lunch with a friend and say, "You won't believe what my husband did this morning," it's an effort to connect with the sisterhood, to be bonded with my friend in the joint incredulity of men. But I have taken a vow of faithfulness to my husband above all others, and I have just broken that vow by telling something about him that he probably did not authorize. So this seemingly benign gossip can turn out to be not so innocent. This may not seem like a big deal, but it has sown two bad seeds. The first is that my friend now has a new, negative lens through which to look at my husband. Second, I have used my words to speak ill when in the same space in time and with the same breath, I could have spoken words that uplifted by husband, bringing goodness into the world.

None of us wants to feel left out. Laura points out, "The hardest thing for me to tame about my mouth is wanting to join in the gossip going on around me at work. Sometimes it starts with factual information, but it can lead to rumors and innuendo if not thwarted." Sometimes we gossip to turn attention (our own and others) away from our own flaws and shortcomings. If I talk about the defects in other people, I don't have to look at mine! In the end, this short-circuits our lives by helping us stay dishonest about who we are.

Sometimes we gossip to show off what we know. A seemingly innocent practice is bringing before your prayer group as a "prayer request" a choice morsel you have discovered about someone you all know. "I just found out this week that Julie and Mark are getting a divorce because he has been cheating on her with her cousin. So we need to pray for them." Julie and Mark do indeed need prayer. But before we bring something like this before a group, we need to ask Julie and Mark directly if they want others to know about their situation. If they don't, you can hit your knees all you want on your own for intercession. If they do, maybe they can make a written prayer request to the group or be more directly involved in asking for prayer. No matter how well-intentioned our motive when engaging in this practice, it is never right to bring up someone else's need to a group when we have not been authorized to do so.

Benign gossip slips out of our mouths, and we don't really mean to injure someone in the process. Toxic gossip is more overt and intended for hurt and division. It's pretty easy to spot. Toxic gossip is spiteful and often secretive. It is designed to force people to take sides and ruin a reputation, a friendship, or someone's emotional health.

As justified as we might feel when someone has hurt us or when we feel someone is clearly on the wrong side of an issue and we need to gather support, the way of wisdom commands that we keep our mouths quiet until we are truly searching for peace. Any division we have with someone is to be taken up directly with that person. A woman at a seminar once told me her Bible-study group was having a horrific struggle between women who were staying home with their children and those who were working outside the home. She once walked into a room with several members huddled around one particular member, who was strenuously speaking against one of the other members who was not present. The absent member was in the "enemy camp," and the speaking member was gathering support for her position against her sister in Christ. God is less interested where we come down on an issue than how we treat others in the discussion.

Gossip can indeed be truthful, but is it helpful? Does it lead us to a healthy and loving place? There are three ways to handle gossip when it pops up on our radar screen. Halt it, stay quiet, or divert the conversation to something healthier and more nourishing.

Quit It!

Halting gossip when we encounter it is just as important as not gossiping in the first place. Proverbs offers two ways for us to do this. "Gossips can't keep secrets, so never confide in blabbermouths" (20:19 MSG). Don't give confirmed gossips material to spread. Give them no logs for their fires.

Second, Proverbs offers this provocative little piece of advice: "You'll find wisdom on the lips of a person of insight, but the short-sighted needs a slap in the face" (10:13 MSG). While I definitely don't advocate we physically slap the offending gossip, I do suggest we take a proactive stance to calling the foolishness of the gossip's behavior as we see it—in private and with love, of course. Cheryl illustrates how this can be done:

> It's so hard to cut off gossip or break away from it when a person or group starts up. But I try. Recognizing it is the first step.
>
> I work in a public library, and one day one of my colleagues and I were chatting. I don't recall how our conversation came around to this, but the topic of a local homeless-looking woman came up. My co-worker started into a dialog about the unpleasantness of this person whom everyone in the community knows (from a distance). People stare at her and like to talk about her, but few have taken the time to get to know her. I've gotten so tired of hearing people go on about this woman, who isn't poor; she's just got really poor hygiene. It's like she doesn't believe in washing or wearing clean clothes. She's apparently well off financially; you can often see her gripping a handful of dollars as she heads away from her bank or into the local bakery. She's intelligent. Her daily routine includes a trip to the library to read the daily papers and browse through the nonfiction section a while.
>
> I knew just what was coming as my work buddy started

> up. "It's like when Margaret (not her real name) comes in..." I thought, *Who are we to judge her or treat her differently than we're expected to treat any other customer?* This time I told my colleague, "I don't want to talk about Margaret. She's a nice person. I like talking with her and helping her out when I can. In fact, I consider her a friend."
>
> I was hoping she would just stop, change the subject, but she kept on. "I know, but..."
>
> "Listen," I said. "I really don't want to hear this." This was the first time I had the courage to point-blank cut off someone's gossip. I guess I'm usually worried I'll be the next topic. It was uncomfortable, but a little easier because it was a one-on-one situation, not a group. I was pleased to see my colleague let it go without either of us getting angry and storming off. While I typically fear a person will hold a grudge if I take action like this, this time the awkwardness quickly subsided, and we continue to work well together as if it hadn't happened. I give my colleague credit for not taking offense, as I might have if the tables were turned and I was the blabbermouth. Best case scenario: My reaction will make her think twice before she speaks negatively about Margaret again, and I am bolstered to refrain from starting and participating in gossip more often.

Steer Clear

A second way to handle gossip is to decide ahead of time you won't participate. Setting boundaries in this regard can be a little lonely. E E Cummings observed, "To be nobody but yourself—in a world which is doing its best, night and day, to make you everybody else—means to fight the hardest battle which any human being can fight, and never stop fighting." One of my former colleagues shared her experience in her current workplace:

> My workplace is such a swirl of gossip and negativity, and I noticed this on my first day at my job over six years ago. Because of that, I have made a conscious decision not to participate in the gossip and try the best I can to deflect

> the negativity from my life. At the same time I have made a concerted effort to always be polite and kind and helpful. Setting boundaries is not easy! As a result, I am basically shunned by the other secretaries I work with. That makes work a difficult place. I won't say I hate my job because I am really fulfilled by the actual work I do. Let's just say this place and the way I choose to handle it doesn't do much for one's self-esteem. However, when I go home at night and when I get up in the morning, I can look at myself in the mirror and know I am remaining true to the person I am supposed to be. Yes, my job situation is difficult and sometimes unpleasant, but I continue to tell myself I'm standing up for the right thing.

There are definite trade-offs for setting boundaries, and you may find you're not very popular for what you decide. Yet two of the greatest benefits of setting good boundaries are attracting more healthy people into your life and participating in more energizing and life-giving activities. Gossip is an area in which we need to make definite decisions about what we stand for and what we won't stand for, and then lovingly and firmly set our boundaries.

The Old Diversion Tactic

My friend Myra offers this proactive option for handling gossip when it pops into her life:

> Eleanor Roosevelt said, "Great minds discuss ideas. Average minds discuss events. Small minds discuss people." I think of this often when I'm tempted to tell others what I've heard about people. It's hard to resist, however, when others in a conversation are on that path. Often at parties or family gatherings I realize the majority of the conversation is gossip. I do my best to talk about what others in my life or in my presence did that was true: telling childhood stories, for example. I'll talk about my children and ask about theirs. I'll share stories about my professional work and ask about theirs. If that doesn't work and I can't get others engaged

> in any other type of conversation, I talk about the weather or move on.

When it comes to gossip and the giving of grace and compassion, Christ offered a smart and time-tested rule that has never failed yet: "Here is a simple rule-of-thumb guide for behavior: Ask yourself what you want people to do for you, then grab the initiative and do it for them. Add up God's Law and Prophets and this is what you get" (Matthew 7:12 MSG).

My Internet tea buddy, Denise, shared with me two examples from her own life of women who have learned to harness this habit.

> Believe it or not, my 17-year-old daughter comes to mind when I think of an example of wise speech. She does not participate in gossip or trashing of "friends." She is weary of many of her classmates because of their habit of talking about those who aren't present. She never adds to news I share about difficulties others are having...even when she has what could be thought to be "the scoop" on others. She keeps prayer requests silent and private. She shares what truly will benefit others and not harm them.
>
> My grandmother, now deceased, was another example for me. She never said an unkind word about anyone. She comes to mind when I have a choice before me to share a prayer request that has private details with a mutual friend or not at all.

As one of my favorite modern-day smart mouths Mary Engelbreit quoted in her 1999 Proverbial Calendar for the month of March—

> There's so much good in the worst of us
> And so much bad in the best of us
> It ill behooves any of us
> To talk about the rest of us.

I appreciate the sweet simplicity my other friend named Mary uses as she comments on gossip: "Less is better, none is good. I'm getting there."

No Trash Talk

The book of Proverbs has a couple warnings about trashy talk. "Put away perversity from your mouth; keep corrupt talk far from your lips" (Proverbs 4:24). "The lips of the righteous know what is fitting, but the mouth of the wicked only what is perverse" (Proverbs 10:32). "Perverse" is the common word, and it has lots of descriptive cousins. The thesaurus offers "deviant, wrong, warped, corrupt, wicked, depraved, perverted, immoral, degenerate, evil, bad, nasty." That's a mouthful.

Unfortunately being crass or vulgar is one sure way to get people's attention. Teenagers do it all the time because it makes grownups sit up and take notice. Sometimes we use coarse or gross language because we "want to get the point across." But the point we end up making could very well be different than the one we intended to make! I love the succinct way my friend Cheryl puts it: "I like to pass on the advice my husband grew up with. His mom would say people who use cuss words come off as not being intelligent enough to know the right words to complete sentences. Cussing makes you sound dumb."

Ephesians 5:4 counsels, "Nor should there be obscenity, foolish talk or coarse joking, which are out of place, but rather thanksgiving." My friend Becky calls it having a "potty mouth," and she believes this is one of the hardest areas in which to maintain a smart mouth. It's difficult because it's so often not considered that big a deal or an offense in our culture. It's certainly not like hurting someone with lies, harsh criticism, or thoughtless gossip. It's a victimless crime.

Some of us talk coarsely because it's what we did before we began the transformation into the likeness of Jesus. Some of us talk this way because our families did when we were growing up. Some of us talk this way because we get fed up with trying to be good all the time. Whatever the reason, it evokes a startling image in Proverbs 11:22: "Like a gold ring in a pig's snout is a beautiful woman who shows no discretion." Attractiveness is not just physical. We are all meant to be attractive. And we are all to make the teachings of Christ attractive

(Titus 2:9-10). But we'll end up looking as foolish as a pig wearing jewelry if we aren't decorous in the way we speak.

My friend Catherine talks about the ways crass language can unravel the threads of relationship-building, as she experienced with one of her high school teachers:

> My French teacher in high school had learned his French during the war. It was colorful! He also taught Spanish, which I had studied a little previous to taking French. He could and would swear in three languages. I complained to my father numerous times, but my father informed me this was my battle and I needed to handle it. I went to the teacher and told him I found it offensive. He basically told me that was the way he was, and I could take it or leave it. The conversation was less than satisfying.
>
> I did notice as time went on that he didn't swear in class as much as he did when I started.

My friend Jay has a unique way to draw attention to and stimulate discussion about foul and vulgar language:

> In our family there is a $1 charge for each foul word that is spoken. This fee is charged to visitors and family alike. The first person to identify the use of the word is the keeper of the $1. At times (usually during long trips) we allow free time of one minute using any word that one chooses. We have found that often the time is spent more in laughter than in the use of foul language, and we seem to always have a discussion of why some words are foul and inappropriate to use.

Crass talk also inhibits the growth of community because, as my friend Laura puts it, "Foul language turns people off, and they stop listening." If people aren't listening to each other, they can't get to know each other, they can't work out their differences, they can't make plans necessary to help bring God's hopes and dreams to his creation. That's a pretty steep price to pay for not caring enough to watch our language!

Morsels to Chew On

1. Has anyone ever gossiped about you? How did it affect your relationship? What did you do with the experience?

2. Is there ever a time when gossip may be acceptable and helpful? What is the difference, in your experience, between benign gossip and toxic gossip?

3. How can you recognize when you are about to gossip? Are there particular situations in which you are more tempted to gossip than in others? What internal need are you trying to fill? Is there another avenue for filling that need?

4. What will your tactic be to stop the people in your life who gossip?

5. On a scale of 1 to 10 with 1 being crystal clear and 10 being sewer sludge, how clean is your talk and your language? What needs to happen to move you more toward a 1?

Dear God, gossip hurts. Please forgive me for the times I have done it. Please help me forgive others for the times I have been hurt by it. Help me resist the temptation to be in the in-crowd or to make myself feel better by talking about the misfortunes of others. Let my speech be upright and positive so I will bring strength and dignity to others.

I want to season my conversation with grace, realizing that foul language and coarse talk are not indicative of a wise and loving person. Help me be sensitive to your Holy Spirit so I can hear you when you remind me to watch my mouth.

In Christ's name, amen.

Example is not the main thing when influencing others. It is the only thing.

Albert Schweitzer

13

Smart Mouth on the Move

Justice is truth in action.

Joseph Joubert

Our mouths are always at their smartest when we are using them to bring good into the world for other people. These are the threads of advocacy, compassion, and justice that King Lemuel's mother was weaving into the fabric of community when she said, "Speak up for those who cannot speak for themselves, for the rights of all who are destitute. Speak up and judge fairly; defend the rights of the poor and needy" (Proverbs 31:8-9).

Your speech is supremely wise when you use God's gift of your tongue to do the work of the Lord. Many people in our world, because of handicap, age, or social disparity cannot speak for themselves. Or if they can and do, they are dismissed because they are perceived to be inferior or ineffective by those who have the power to change the situations of those who plead.

You're an advocate when you're willing to stay at the task of speaking up for people. A beautiful and somewhat poignant story of advocacy is found in Genesis 18. Abraham is an advocate for his nephew, Lot, in the infamous city of Sodom, in which Lot lives:

> Abraham confronted [God], "Are you serious? Are you planning on getting rid of the good people right along with the bad? What if there are fifty decent people left in the city; will you lump the good with the bad and get rid of the lot? Wouldn't you spare the city for the sake of those fifty innocents? I can't believe you'd do that, kill off the good and the bad alike as if there were no difference between them. Doesn't the Judge of all the Earth judge with justice?"
>
> God said, "If I find fifty decent people in the city of Sodom, I'll spare the place just for them."
>
> Abraham came back, "Do I, a mere mortal made from a handful of dirt, dare open my mouth again to my Master? What if the fifty fall short by five—would you destroy the city because of those missing five?"
>
> He said, "I won't destroy it if there are forty-five."
>
> Abraham spoke up again, "What if you only find forty?"
>
> "Neither will I destroy it if for forty."
>
> He said, "Master, don't be irritated with me, but what if only thirty are found?"
>
> "No, I won't do it if I find thirty."
>
> He pushed on, "I know I'm trying your patience, Master, but how about for twenty?"
>
> "I won't destroy it for twenty."
>
> He wouldn't quit, "Don't get angry, Master—this is the last time. What if you only come up with ten?"
>
> "For the sake of ten, I won't destroy the city."
>
> When God finished talking with Abraham, he left. And Abraham went home (verses 23-33 msg).

Well, you may know how the story ends. God couldn't find even ten decent people in the city of Sodom and the city was destroyed. But Abraham showed some pluck, didn't he? As an advocate, he was bold, compassionate, and tenacious. He was talking to the God of the universe! We could take a few lessons from him.

Jesus thought advocacy was pretty important too. In the prayer recorded in the gospel of John just before his arrest, Jesus acted as an advocate for his disciples and then for all believers. It is some of the most beautiful writing in Scripture:

> I will remain in the world no longer, but they are still in the world, and I am coming to you. Holy Father, protect them by the power of your name—the name you gave me—so that they may be one as we are one. While I was with them, I protected them and kept them safe by that name you gave me. None has been lost except the one doomed to destruction so that Scripture would be fulfilled.
>
> I am coming to you now, but I say these things while I am still in the world, so that they may have the full measure of my joy within them. I have given them your word and the world has hated them, for they are not of the world any more than I am of the world. My prayer is not that you take them out of the world but that you protect them from the evil one. They are not of the world, even as I am not of it. Sanctify them by the truth; your word is truth. As you sent me into the world, I have sent them into the world. For them I sanctify myself, that they too may be truly sanctified.
>
> My prayer is not for them alone. I pray also for those who will believe in me through their message, that all of them may be one, Father, just as you are in me and I am in you. May they also be in us so that the world may believe that you have sent me. I have given them the glory that you gave me, that they may be one as we are one: I in them and you in me. May they be brought to complete unity to let the world know that you sent me and have loved them even as you have loved me.
>
> Father, I want those you have given me to be with me where I am, and to see my glory, the glory you have given me because you loved me before the creation of the world.
>
> Righteous Father, though the world does not know you, I know you, and they know that you have sent me. I have made you known to them, and will continue to make you known in order that the love you have for me may be in them and that I myself may be in them (17:11-26).

Jesus is our advocate so we know what we need to about our relationship with him and what God desires for us. In truly understanding this love, we are enabled to be advocates for others.

Jesus went a step further. He told his disciples in this moving final conversation that he would send them their own advocate: "And I will ask the Father, and he will give you another Advocate, to be with you forever. This is the Spirit of truth, whom the world cannot receive, because it neither sees him nor knows him. You will know him, because he abides with you, and he will be in you" (John 14:16-17 NRSV). "Advocate" is also translated "helper" or "counselor."

Who in your world cannot speak for themselves? Who is in need of mercy, justice, assistance, and love? Are you called to be a champion for the children of your church before a governing body? Maybe you are to promote the rights of someone you love as she lies dying or is in need of medical treatment. Does your elderly neighbor need an ally? Do the refugees you see on television need an advocate? What's happening in the downtown area of your city or town? Is there a need for you to speak up for the rights of the poor, the undereducated, the imprisoned?

I want to introduce you to three remarkable advocates, each with a story and a unique point about advocacy.

Sally is a hospice nurse. If you've never been around a hospice professional, I encourage you to put that high on the list of things to do in the next month or so. You will find a person of deep spiritual strength—a person who is continually standing in the gap between this life and the next. You will find a person who is connected to the realities of life and death, the human and the divine.

> It's interesting how much advocacy and listening are connected in my mind. I think about patients I see being treated in the hospital. The first thing one has to do is go in and listen to them, to truly hear their story. In the story you discover that often they know that treatment is futile and what they really want is to stop that treatment. Then, as the

advocate, it's just a matter of telling their story with them and for them.

On the other hand, if you find that they want to fight to the end, advocacy is a matter of respecting that and asking how the hospice team can support them in that fight.

But you can't advocate for someone if you don't know their story.

Sometimes we don't feel very powerful because of temperament or because of who we might have to speak to. Sally shared this too:

> There is nothing more terrifying to an introvert than the idea of speaking up—even in defense of someone who is in need. As an introvert, speaking in front of a group of people, even my friends and peers, is paralyzing. However, there are times when the terror needs to be set aside and we must find the courage to speak up and defend what we believe in.
>
> I believe in my son, Alex. He is one of the strongest people I have ever met—determined, bright, with a heart that is open to God. He has struggled in school since first grade, and now he is a sophomore. Every teacher has told us the same thing. He is very bright, he knows the material, his hand is always up in class. For some reason, this knowledge does not come across in tests and written assignments. We have, over the years, explored many reading interventions, eye therapy, and tutors. Still, his grades do not reflect his knowledge. Every year, since third grade, I have requested testing to determine if there is a learning disability, and every year that request has been denied.
>
> Last week we had a meeting at school. I pushed and pushed to get this meeting, involving his teachers, principal, intervention specialist, and school psychologist. However, I knew from previous experience what would happen during that meeting. Alex and I would be there together, at a huge table, with "the team." No matter how I try to frame it in my mind, there is always a feeling of us against them—and there are so many of them. At some point in these meetings, I

always feel the tears start to form and my mind start to freeze. I feel overwhelmed and helpless, incapable of defending the person I love. I am blessed to have a wonderful life coach, and I requested some coaching for this situation.

Robin and I discussed the upcoming meeting, the people who would be involved, and the people who would be praying for us while we were in that meeting. It helped immensely to realize just how many people were praying for us. Robin reminded me of the passage in Hebrews that talks about us being surrounded by a "great cloud of witnesses," and as we explored this further, she guided me to a wonderful visual image. It was powerful enough that when Alex and I were sitting at the table and I felt the tears start to form and my mind begin to fog, I could look at the walls and see in my mind's eye that we were surrounded by our own team, much more powerful and much more influential than the people we were sitting at the table with.

We also discussed the individuals who would be around the table. Although we have had years of frustration, this principal and this group of teachers have been a great encouragement to Alex, seeing his potential and going above and beyond to encourage him and help him realize it. It helped immensely to look across the room and remind myself that these teachers are allies, not adversaries.

We left the meeting with a plan in place for Alex to be tested, finally, for learning disabilities. I left the meeting knowing, without a doubt, that we were not there alone.

Now, meet Libby.

I'm an advocate. I didn't plan to be an advocate; I just wanted to give voice for the children who had none. It never seemed fair that the innocent children who had been terribly abused were then being shuffled in and out of foster homes with no way to tell what was really happening in those homes. If I didn't start to speak up for them, who would? So I've started talking and working on making a difference. It is written on my heart and fills my thoughts and priorities. God hears my

> prayers, and when I least expect it or when I've worked really hard at it, I make a new connection toward my dreams of helping foster youth. Each time this happens it is truly amazing.
>
> When my daughter, Katherine, was nine months old, she was diagnosed with life-threatening food allergies to six foods. Just a drop of milk would kill her. As a stay-at-home mom my life was turned upside down. After doing weeks of research I found a support group. And I was amazed that so few people without allergies knew about handling allergies.
>
> So I decided that I would help educate as many people as I could. I attend conferences to better educate myself. I've taught teachers, principals, bus drivers, maintenance workers, friends, and relatives. I have even had the extraordinary experience of helping a friend recognize that her infant was having food allergy reactions and helped her find a doctor. To me, being an advocate can be giving a voice to those without one, and it can mean helping to educate others. But it always means "passion." I have a deep passion for both areas and each makes my heart sing when I'm able to help others.

These remarkable women are intentional advocates. They have distinct populations for whom they are champions. They have identifiable passions and causes. They are truly inspirational to be around.

Finally I would like you to get to know Linda. One of the things I love about Linda is that she doesn't really think of herself as an advocate. Just by her presence in any group or any situation she is an advocate. While many people are advocates for specific populations or causes, Linda is an advocate for justice. She is interested in justice, openness, inclusion, and the destruction of boundaries that make some people feel like insiders and some feel like outsiders. She can and does speak up in groups, often reluctantly by her own admission. But she moves in and through life "like a disquieting voice muttering truths that maybe aren't very pleasant or comfortable."

Advocates can be like the prophets described in Scripture. Sometimes when we are advocates we may experience frustration and being misunderstood. As Linda observes, this is "related to that of various prophets, minor prophets, and lesser speakers of unpleasant truth." Linda observes that it is indeed a gift, sometimes more of an irritating compulsion, and certainly something she would like to give back every so often.

Of all the ways to use our smart mouths, perhaps advocacy comes closest to the heart of God's hopes and dreams for his creation. There are also times when we may not set out to be an advocate on a given day, yet the opportunity to have a smart mouth on the move presents itself spontaneously. I call this being an "accidental advocate."

A friend told me of an experience she had in a local large grocery store. She was standing in a regular, non-express checkout line that was positioned next to the 15-items-or-less express line. She witnessed the clerk asking a gentleman who was in the express line if he had more than 15 items. His response was, "Who are you, the warden?" She pointed out to him that the line he was in was an express lane, and because there were other customers behind him in line, his violation was holding them up. His reply was, "I have been coming to this store for years. Of course I know this is an express line." He then tossed his check-cashing card at her and revealed to her that he was a personal friend of the prominent owner of this particular grocery chain.

All in all, my friend was disgusted by the customer's rude and arrogant behavior, and she felt sorry for the clerk. Once the man had left, my friend tapped the clerk on the shoulder to assure her that at least someone else knew what had happened—that this man had been inappropriate and the clerk had handled the situation as well as she could. The grateful clerk asked if my friend would relay the story to the manager because she was fearful that the man would call the store and try to get her fired.

My friend used the power of speech to be an advocate for the clerk—someone she didn't even know—who needed a voice to speak up on her behalf. Advocacy can be that simple.

I've put advocacy near the end of our Smart Mouth discussion because it encompasses so many of the other traits, experiences, and outcomes we've looked at throughout this book. To be an advocate requires great love and wisdom. You need to listen, to know yourself well, to be honest, and to be willing to get involved in conflict. An advocate learns to forgive the bullies and encourage the downtrodden. An advocate knows to speak of another's story only to the people who are involved (no gossiping).

The responsibility of advocacy is on all of us. Don't wait until you've become accomplished at all the other Smart Mouth traits to step up to the plate for someone else. You can do it out of sheer goodness and a sense of the unfairness of a situation. Search your heart and see if God is asking you to use your smart mouth for justice and advocacy.

"Speak Up" Sound Check

The most profound realities are often the most simple. This Sound Check has only a couple assessments, but they make a deep impact on our communities if we use our smart mouths in these ways. Respond to the statements using the following scale:

5=ALWAYS 4=OFTEN 3=SOMETIMES 2=RARELY 1=NEVER

____ 1. I recognize injustice in my community (family, neighborhood, city, and beyond) and speak up for those who are oppressed.

____ 2. I continually monitor my everyday surroundings and stand up for people who are being treated poorly.

How close are you to 10? Just being aware that you want to be more aware will make you a better candidate for having a smart mouth. You'll begin to see things you haven't noticed before and perhaps start to feel God's nudges in ways you've not experienced. A perfect 10 is definitely what we're shooting for on this scale.

Morsels to Chew On

1. What is your reaction to Abraham's interaction with God?

2. Reflect on the words Jesus spoke to his Father on our behalf. What do they mean to you?

3. What does it mean to you that an advocate (the Holy Spirit) has been sent to live in you?

4. Who in your world can't speak for themselves or have been dismissed by others because of age, class, race, or gender? What are their situations? What do they need? How can you be their advocate?

Gracious and compassionate God, in speaking out for the rights of those who can't, I become as close to your heart as I can be. Your hopes and dreams for your creation are centered in compassion, justice, and the wholeness and welfare of all. When I'm an advocate, I join you in fulfilling Christ's mission that all will have life and have it abundantly.

Forgive the times when I am indifferent to unfairness, needs, and sadness. Forgive the times I am caught up in my own world to the extent that I forget your heart. Enable me to see and speak up for the situations and the people that need your touch and your love in very tangible ways. Make me aware of where you need me as I listen to the passions of my heart and discern the unique call you have on my life.

In Christ's name, amen.

A man is selfish not for pursuing his own
good, but for neglecting his neighbor's.

Richard Whately

14

The Wisdom of Silence

Better to remain silent and be thought a fool,
than to speak out and remove all doubt.

Abraham Lincoln

Now comes the nitty-gritty that's been hinted at in several chapters of this book. Sometimes the best way to have a smart mouth is *to keep it shut.* This chapter's opening quote is a wryly humorous paraphrase of Proverbs 17:27-28: "A man of knowledge uses words with restraint, and a man of understanding is even-tempered. Even a fool is thought wise if he keeps silent, and discerning if he holds his tongue." As my wise and clever friend Libby quips, "I need to remember that every thought traveling through my mind does not need to exit my mouth!"

Being quiet can keep us out of trouble. When we take time to be quiet, we have a chance to truly weigh the benefits and costs of what we intend to say. "When in doubt, don't" is a piece of folk advice I follow (although probably not often enough) when it comes to speaking or not. Any of us can look over our lives and rue the idiotic, cruel, misguided, and silly things we've said. But if we can get a better handle on having a smart mouth that is quiet, many future tears and sleepless nights may be avoided.

Being quiet gives us more opportunities to listen. We can better hear God's Spirit, the inner workings of our own perceptions and motives, and others when we're not concentrating on being heard ourselves. Throughout the book of Proverbs we are encouraged to embrace instruction (1:8), pay attention to experienced teachers (12:15), walk with the wise (13:20), seek counsel and sound advice (15:22), seek knowledge with our ears (18:15), and listen to the law (28:9). These pieces of advice are enabled through the kind of listening that is best done when we use restraint in our speech. Perhaps this is why some observe wisely that we each have one mouth and two ears.

Aldous Huxley said, "Silence is as full of potential wisdom and wit as the unhewn marble of great sculpture." Being restrained in speech can clear the path for hearing the voice of God. One day as I was preparing to send out my weekly Soul Snack message to my email list, I asked my son, Grant, 11 years old at the time, what I should offer to readers that day that would make their lives better for the week. He sat quietly for a moment and then said, "Tell them to block out the world for a moment of silence to look inside themselves and listen for one thing they're good at." Such wise words from one so young!

Let's explore some very good reasons to be quiet, to use discretion in self-disclosure, and look at two situations in which many of us are quiet but might need to be more vocal.

Taking the Long View

We can exercise restraint in being negative as evidenced by this funny little story that circulated on the Internet:

> For 50 years Uncle Jack left the box alone...until Aunt Edna was old and dying. One day when he was putting their affairs in order, he found the box again and thought it might hold something important.
>
> Opening it, he found two doilies and $2,500 in cash. He took the box to her and asked about the contents.
>
> "My mother gave me that box the day we married," she explained. "She told me to make a doily to help ease my frustrations every time I got mad at you."

Uncle Jack was very touched that in 50 years she'd only been mad at him twice.

"What's the $2,500 for?" he asked.

"Oh, that's the money I made selling the doilies," she answered.

Aunt Edna believed the advice Harlan Miller offers: "Often the difference between a successful marriage and a mediocre one consists of leaving three or four things a day unsaid." Aunt Edna's strategy is best used when you have made a conscious decision to not hold any grudges and to honestly not be bothered by whatever the irritants might be. If you can make that kind of decision and harbor no malice, restraining from consistently voicing aggravation for common frustrations may make the long haul of life much easier to enjoy.

We Will *Never* Agree

My friend Laura disagrees with her husband on most political situations. But since she is an avid advocate of using discretion and restraint when jumping into discussions where you already know there is very little chance for agreement, her marriage is very solid. This is a variation on one of the themes we saw in chapter 7 on resolving conflict: agree to disagree. There is quiet maturity in staying away from topics that are historically hotbeds of conflict with no possible resolution. In almost every intimate relationship the people involved recognize over time the issues that are better left untouched. They are usually topics of opinion or perspective that don't affect the quality of the relationship.

If you have a disagreement of opinion or perspective with someone and you both find it entertaining to keep talking about it, then by all means have fun. But if you have a disagreement that always ends in frustration and hurt feelings, it's best to avoid those topics. Hopefully, you have plenty of other things to talk about.

Wrong Side of the Bed

I have known my feisty friend Tiffany since she was 15 years old.

She's been close to me and my family for years—to the extent that she even was a nanny for my daughter, Madison. Tiffany is now the mother of three kids. She's still pretty fiery. She told me a story in which she used restraint, although her lip probably bled from her biting it. She was responding to my weekly "Soul Snack for Zesty Living" email in which I had mentioned a quote by Ariel and Will Durant: "One of the lessons of history is that nothing is often a good thing to do and always a clever thing to say."

> OK, so you were the good little angel sitting on my shoulder on Sunday! We went to my niece's baptism, and afterward my sister had lunch at the church. One of her friends, very bossy and overbearing I might add, had taken control of lunch and was making sure everything was in place. I pretty much got pushed out of the kitchen. After lunch I decided I was going to help clear up. This other lady was doing circles around me and being obnoxious because of her need to be in control. I put the lids back on the desserts. Lunch was over and people were leaving. This very bossy woman looked at me and in a very demanding tone said, "You can take those lids right back off the desserts because I didn't get any!" Yes, I bit my lip and didn't say a word, but I did want to look at this grown-up and tell her that manners would have been more acceptable and appreciated. I took the lids off and walked out of the kitchen.

Tiffany encountered someone who was obviously cranky and not very interested in building the fabric of community through friendship. I know Tiffany, and I'm guessing she wasn't feeling really loving at the moment she walked out of the kitchen...but she was acting wisely. We may not always be feeling angelic while we're cultivating our smart mouths, but we can still act and speak (or not speak) with discretion and wait for our feelings to catch up with our actions.

When you encounter someone who is having a bad day, make use of this wise observation: "It takes one fool to backtalk and two fools to make a conversation of it." Sometimes we just have to let it go.

Oh, the Look

My friend and director of a ministry to abused women and children, Linda Crissman, was formerly a teacher and trainer in classroom management.

> One of the most important tools I taught teachers is "calm is strength." Learning to say nothing and using your body language to show you mean business was the principle behind the program. It was amazing what happened in the schools that used the program.
>
> The emotionally handicapped kids who came into my program were considered the worst in the county, yet they were well behaved with me. A therapist asked them why. Every one of the kids told her they were afraid of my eyes! She said, "You mean when she yells at you?" The kids responded, "Oh, she never yells. It's worse. She says nothing, and then she looks at you!" Yes, saying nothing is very powerful indeed!

If you know from experience that your nonverbals are going to carry more weight than your verbals, you can use restraint in your speech and build community and relationships in this way. Most parents understand this!

"SHHHH" SOUND CHECK

Sometimes the best thing to say is nothing at all! Respond to the statements using the following scale:

5=ALWAYS 4=OFTEN 3=SOMETIMES 2=RARELY 1=NEVER

____ 1. I choose to be quiet so I can listen more effectively.

____ 2. I choose to be quiet when I know speaking will make a situation more tense.

____ 3. I know with whom I have long-standing disagreements, and we've agreed to disagree.

____ 4. I know the power of nonverbals and use them appropriately.

____ 5. I know when I'm tempted to talk just to impress others, and I choose to be quiet at those times.

____ 6. I appropriately self-disclose.

____ 7. I don't use silence as a weapon.

____ 8. I don't keep dangerous secrets.

The scale for this Sound Check is 8 to 40. Scores closer to 40 indicate you're comfortable with silence and know when to speak and when to keep quiet. Others probably see you as wise and self-assured. If your score is lower, what can you do to make peace with yourself so you can be at peace in a variety of situations? Being peaceful with yourself is the foundation that allows you to be peaceful in every situation—negative and positive.

Foolish Talk

Proverbs 10:19-20 (MSG) counsels: "The more talk, the less truth; the wise measure their words. The speech of a good person is worth waiting for; the blabber of the wicked is worthless." Two compelling situations that suggest it's better to be quiet than to speak represent what the apostle Paul may have been referring to by foolish talk in Ephesians 5:4: "Nor should there be obscenity, foolish talk or coarse joking, which are out of place."

Have you ever tried to impress someone only to end up looking like an idiot? I very much wanted to impress the senior minister of the first church I ever served professionally. I was young and eager to show what I knew on lots of subjects. One subject was something I only knew a little bit about, but since my husband was so good at it I figured I probably picked up some of it by osmosis. And that's golf.

The senior minister was an avid golfer. Standing around after a meeting one evening with him and several other people, I said, "So what do you shoot on a, say, par 72 golf course?" I thought all golf courses had different par numbers. He kindly and bemusedly said, "Robin, all standard courses are par 72." Well, I don't know if by the standards of Proverbs I was wicked, but I sure had blabbered. This may seem minor, but I was embarrassed!

Don't speak if you're trying to be impressive and you don't know what you're talking about.

Second, don't speak if you feel compelled to say something in a meeting or gathering just because you think you'll look stupid if you're quiet. Thankfully, no story about myself comes to mind in this category, but I have witnessed it for other people. It's ugly. George Eliot has a humorous and succinct reminder for us: "Blessed is the man who, having nothing to say, abstains from giving us wordy evidence of the fact." And Proverbs 17:28 says, "Even a fool is thought wise if he keeps silent."

Sacred Silence

There will be times in our lives when we need to be silent simply because what we have seen or experienced defies words or expression. These are times of sacred silence as we ponder the meaning, savor the communion with God, and wait until, possibly, it's time to share later. Peter, James, and John experienced such a time when they accompanied Jesus on one of his prayer trips into the mountains:

> [Jesus] climbed the mountain to pray, taking Peter, John, and James along. While he was in prayer, the appearance of his face changed and his clothes became blinding white. At once two men were there talking with him. They turned out to be Moses and Elijah—and what a glorious appearance they made! They talked over his exodus, the one Jesus was about to complete in Jerusalem.
>
> Meanwhile, Peter and those with him were slumped over in sleep. When they came to, rubbing their eyes, they saw Jesus in his glory and the two men standing with him. When Moses and Elijah had left, Peter said to Jesus, "Master, this is a great moment! Let's build three memorials: one for you, one for Moses, and one for Elijah." He blurted this out without thinking.

> While he was babbling on like this, a light-radiant cloud enveloped them. As they found themselves buried in the cloud, they became deeply aware of God. Then there was a voice out of the cloud: "This is my Son, the Chosen! Listen to him."
>
> When the sound of the voice died away, they saw Jesus there alone. They were speechless. And they continued speechless, said not one thing to anyone during those days of what they had seen (Luke 9:28-36 MSG).

We live in a very verbal culture. Everyone seems sure they should say everything about anything they are experiencing. Sacred silence can do wonders for us in our development as people who have something worthwhile to say at the right time. When we take time and give attention to the possibility of sacred silence, we connect with the wonderful source of all that is worth talking about, the source of our wisdom and love, the source of the best hopes and dreams for creation—Jesus.

Sharing Yourself with Others

In chapter 10, Threads of Forgiveness, we explored wise confession when it comes to asking forgiveness from others for wrongs we've done to them through an act of will or negligence. When we talk about wise confession in this chapter, we're referring to the art of self-disclosure. Self-disclosure is telling someone something they don't already know about you. A wise person knows self-disclosure is key to developing relationships and strengthening the fabric of community. But there is also the best time to say things, specific people to share with, and the knowledge of how much to reveal. Several factors determine wise disclosure.

Your temperament. By nature some of us are more open with what is going on with us. Some of us are more reserved. Figure out where your comfort zone is, and then move in and out of this zone as you sense is appropriate.

Your culture. You may be from an ethnic, economic, or family culture that teaches it's better to "play things close to the vest" or keep more information to yourself. You may be from a culture that "lets it all hang out." How much you choose to self-disclose is initially influenced by this culture.

Your listeners. Your degree of self-disclosure is definitely dependent on your listeners. The context of your conversation has a great deal to say about how much information you want to or should tell the receivers. An intimate gathering of people you trust will bring out different information than when you're with a party of people you are just getting acquainted with. While this sounds obvious, you may have been exposed to someone who has trouble distinguishing the sometimes subtle differences with results that range from mildly uncomfortable to downright embarrassing or inappropriate.

Your topic. You may feel very comfortable talking about family matters with nearly everyone, but financial topics are definitely off-limits. You get to decide. You are in charge of your mouth. Avoid being influenced to speak about topics you don't wish to speak about simply because the rest of the conversation leans that way. People with smart mouths know who they are, what their limits are, and how they will feel about themselves if those limits are violated.

When Silence Isn't Golden

There are two compelling instances when silence is not helpful and it's time to grow up and speak up. The first is when we are tempted to give someone "the silent treatment." This type of communication (although it may seem like noncommunication) is a weapon. Weapons are not helpful in building community. The silent treatment is different from the request for recess we looked at as a conflict resolution tool in chapter 6. While a request for recess is meant to be an ultimately cooperative tool to establish space for thinking things through and not saying things in the heat of a moment, the silent treatment is designed to manipulate the other person into chasing us, begging us, or escalating their emotions to frustrate them into seeing things our way. It usually doesn't get us closer to the kind of positive conflict resolution we explored in chapter 7.

The second instance when silence isn't golden is when we're keeping inappropriate secrets. These secrets aren't the same as using discretion with private information or not letting your sister know there's a surprise birthday party being planned for her. How can you tell if a secret is tearing holes in the fabric of community? We all have a right to keep certain things to ourselves. In fact, discernment often guides us to this conclusion. Yet an inappropriate secret is going to have some of the following characteristics that are not healthy to anyone:

1. An inappropriate secret bothers the keeper physically and mentally. The fear, anxiety, and shame cause harm to the keeper.
2. An inappropriate secret is something you fear you can't tell *anyone* about.
3. An inappropriate secret is something you fear will be discovered.
4. An inappropriate secret feels like a heavy burden.

Anita Kelly, author of *The Psychology of Secrets* says the most common secrets are about sex. Next on the list are mental health problems and failure, such as losing a job.[1] Addictions and self-destructive behaviors of all sorts are often the subject of secrets.

The community building power of not being silent about secrets is courageously offered by Frederick Buechner in his book *Telling Secrets:*

> I not only have my secrets, I am my secrets. And you are your secrets, too. Our secrets are human secrets, and our trusting each other has as much to do with the secret of what it is to be human.[2]

Dr. Buechner knows what he's talking about. When Frederick

was ten years old his alcoholic father committed suicide and none of the family members went to the funeral. No one spoke of his father again for years.

As Frederick grew, got married, and had a family, he was further plunged into the darkness of secrets as he faced the reality of his daughter's anorexia. His book *Telling Secrets* describes an honest journey in healing through telling the truth to oneself, and then sharing the truth about oneself with others. His wisdom and honesty that strengthen the threads of community come through in what can be a model for all of us as we're deciding how to tell our own secrets wisely without gossiping about the secrets of others:

> I will not try to tell my daughter's story for two reasons. One is that it is not mine to tell but hers. The other is that of course I do not know her story, not the real story, the inside story, of what it was like for her. For the same reasons I will not try to tell what it was like for my wife or our other two children, each of whom in her own way was involved in that story. I can tell only my part in it, what happened to me, and even there I can't be sure I have it right because in many ways it is happening still.[3]

When Nothing Is the Best Thing to Say

As sure as the next breath we take it will happen. Probably sometime this week in fact. You will be faced with a choice to say something or refrain from saying something. It may be a situation with a spouse or a significant other. The moment may arise at work with a boss or colleague. The opportunity may even appear in a grocery store or at a checkout counter. If you have children, it will most certainly show up there when dealing with them.

The chances we have to make wise contributions to our community through our speech are sometimes disguised as moments to simply be quiet. You may have already experienced this. Can you recall a moment in which you're glad you said nothing when you could have said something? And if you haven't ever had a moment in which you wish you had said nothing when you said something, I need you to contact me. I've never met anyone like you!

The gentle nudge of the Holy Spirit will sometimes ask you to be very clever by being very quiet. This takes wisdom, discernment, and restraint on your part. God will help you!

Morsels to Chew On

1. Reflect on a time when you could have said something but didn't. What was the situation? What was the outcome?

2. How can heartfelt and gracious restraint aid long-term relationships? What relationship might benefit from this in your life?

3. Nearly everyone has someone in their life with whom they have a disagreement of opinion or perspective that is so ingrained it's useless to keep talking about it. In your situations, how could you best employ the notion to agree to disagree?

4. Describe a situation in which the positive use of nonverbal communication would be more powerful than the use of verbal communication. Have you experienced this?

5. What advice would you give about when to speak and when to keep quiet to make the best impression?

6. When have you experienced the need or desire for sacred silence? How would talking have changed the mood?

7. How are you at self-disclosure? What do you need to watch out for?

8. What is the difference between using discretion and keeping inappropriate secrets?

9. How is silence not the absence of communication but another powerful expression of it?

Loving and quiet God, many thanks for the gift of quiet. I thank you for the times it has saved me from making verbal mistakes. I praise you for the times it enabled me to really listen to you and to someone else.

Give me wise discernment about when to speak and when to be quiet. Help me be deeply attentive to the Holy Spirit so I will have the presence of heart and mind to listen to your moment-by-moment instructions. Give me the will to use quiet for good and not for harm.

Thank you for the times when I sense you are quiet with me, relaxing and rejoicing in our relationship, in the silence of deep and understanding friendship.

In Christ's name, amen.

The most silent people are generally those
who think most highly of themselves.

William Hazlitt

The Power of Words

Words kill, words give life; they're either poison or fruit—you choose.

Proverbs 18:21 msg

Words do indeed have the power to kill or give life. Some cultures believe words are just as real and alive as animals, plants, and humans. They believe that when a word is spoken, it goes out into the world causing life or death, hurt or healing. William Barclay points out in his commentary on the gospel of John:

> To the Jew a word was far more than a mere sound; it was something which had an independent existence and which actually did things. As Professor John Paterson has put it: "The spoken word to the Hebrew was fearfully alive...It was a unit of energy charged with power. It flies like a bullet to its billet." For that very reason the Hebrew was sparing of words. Hebrew speech has fewer than 10,000; Greek speech has 200,000.[1]

The Hebrews themselves were taking their cue from one of their most significant writings—the book of Genesis. How did we get light, animals, plants, land, sea, sky, and all that's in the sky? God spoke. God's words created. God's words are also cited in the Hebrew culture as a means of destruction.

> See, the Lord is going to lay waste to the earth
> and devastate it;
> he will ruin its face
> and scatter its inhabitants—
> it will be the same
> for priest as for people,
> for master as for servant,
> for mistress as for maid,
> for seller as for buyer,
> for borrower as for lender,
> for debtor as for creditor.
> The earth will be completely laid waste
> and totally plundered.
> The Lord has spoken this word (Isaiah 24:1-3).

Barclay goes on to reiterate the forceful aliveness of words by repeating the findings of his study followed with an interesting story.

> To the people, a word is not merely a sound. It is a power which does things. Once when Sir George Adam Smith was traveling in the desert in the East, a group of Moslems gave his party the customary greeting: "Peace be with you." At the moment, they failed to notice he was a Christian. When they discovered that they had spoken blessing to an infidel, they hurried back to ask the blessing back again. The word was like a thing which could be sent out to do things.[2]

This belief of ancient language explains, Barclay says, why the blessing of Esau, which rightfully belonged to Jacob, could not be taken back. It had already gone out into reality, alive and active, and could not be stopped (Genesis 27:1-40).[3]

When Jesus spoke, his words must have had a living energy of their own. At least twice in John's gospel we read that Jesus' words alone changed people.

> Many of the Samaritans from that town believed in him because of the woman's testimony, "He told me everything I

> ever did." So when the Samaritans came to him, they urged him to stay with them, and he stayed two days. And *because of his words* many more became believers.
>
> They said to the woman, "We no longer believe just because of what you said; now we have heard for ourselves, and we know that this man really is the Savior of the world" (4:39-42).
>
> Even *as he spoke,* many put their faith in him (8:30).

So we too, being created in the image of God, need to speak carefully, for our words do indeed create and our words can indeed destroy.

One very powerful way we communicate is through stories. You've read many stories in this book. The following story from a friend sums up the beauty of a whole community of smart mouths. As you read, pick up the threads of listening, honesty, encouragement, confrontation, forgiveness, restraint, and wisdom. See how the threads of communication with God, with self, and with others are woven together to bring about the essence of God's hopes and dreams for his creation even in the midst of heartache, loss, fear, and separation.

> The story begins with boxes, baggage, and bandages. My husband is a football coach, and we have moved often. Hence the boxes—all the material security blankets; the baggage—all the mental stuff of separation anxiety and leaving special friends and memories; and the bandages—all the wraps and salves of verbal comfort through phone calls, notes, and mostly prayer...until I have healed from the move and am able to embrace my new adventure and find one new friend. It seems like on every life journey stop I have made, one or two friends continue to love me and encourage me from a distance.
>
> In moving far from one dear friend the door opened to six new friends, all of whom love to listen and share encouraging words. I have tried to single out one of them and call her my best friend, but, as in a colorful garden, it takes each flower to make the garden complete and beautiful. In my life garden none of these dear women in Christ could stand alone. We jokingly call ourselves the functional

"Ya- Ya's." We love each other unconditionally. That seldom happens with women. There is almost always a thorn or a big rock in the patch. The beauty of this friendship is that each flower makes for one beautiful centerpiece. These are my sisters in Christ.

I had to leave my friend Tracy on Long Island as I made my new home in Louisville, KY. Now, I'm a southern girl by birth and by the infusion of years of iced tea and fried chicken, so there was a deeply rooted appeal to move south of the Mason–Dixon line where the word "y'all" is understood and accepted as proper English. It was, however, difficult to acknowledge anything good or appealing about this move without my buddy Tracy. Even with the iced tea/y'all appeal, the "woe is me" mantra, tears, pity parties, and dramatic phone calls ranting and wondering how God could move me away from Tracy went on for several months.

Once we moved I had to hide these messy moments of drama from my two school-aged children because they needed to adjust and move on with life. I was the great pretender in front of the children, and they were adjusting beautifully and making great new buddies. Afternoons before the children came home from school were when I struggled the most. Anyone who would listen got an earful about how Tracy was my best friend. We had shared everything: tea, chocolate, driving, the beach, choir, Bible study, and on and on and on. Even our husbands liked each other!

One day, out of nowhere, the phone rang. Tracy's mother was calling from Hawaii. She prayed with me. We prayed for the Lord to bring friends into my life and into Tracy's life. Friends that would heal our hearts and ease the pain of missing each other. (Mind you, I was a grown woman, fretting over my friend like I was in fifth grade.)

The Louisville ladies did not have a choice in becoming my new best friends. They were abruptly blindsided by God and were sent to me directly through prayers being said on the paradise island of Hawaii, the mountains of West Virginia, and the busy streets of Pittsburgh. Power praying by my friend Tracy's mother in Hawaii, my mother in West Virginia, and my mother-in-law in Pittsburgh led me to these lovely Louisville ladies.

If God had warned these unsuspecting women in Louisville of

the 5'1" storm ready to blow into their lives, they would all have tried to make quick bargains with the good Lord. Yet the good news is each of these women opened their hearts and their homes to this needy one. They embraced God's purpose and plan and allowed me, an outsider, to waltz right into their hearts. For the past 15 years they have loved to listen and shared girl talk, mommy moments, encouraging words of love, wisdom, silliness, hope, and faith.

I have always appreciated their friendship. We have great times together. We love each other without pettiness, jealousy, envy, or fear. Our sleepovers don't require morning makeup or hairdos. There is an unexplainable comfort zone among us. I could go on about the good times, the support, the secrets, hopes for our children, our dreams, the small annoyances of our husbands, our hormones or lack thereof, concern for our aging parents, and our faith in a loving God.

You have your own remarkable friend stories. Yours are special to you and you don't need ours, but I do want to share with you what makes these blindsided belles so important to my life journey.

Several years later I had another move to Columbus, Ohio, taking me away from my Louisville friends. Seven months ago my husband had a heart attack, five stents, three balloons, and one big ugly Stage IV renal clear cell carcinoma diagnosis with metastases. This life-altering hospital experience happened in a matter of five short days and five long nights. Many of us have our own version of flashbulb memory moments. It may not have been cancer; it may have been a car accident, a lost job, an unfaithful spouse, too much debt, a rebellious child, an unforgiving friend, death, or depression. The point is we have all to some degree in some way encountered a gut-wrenching experience that is our worst nightmare. One can't change it, and one can't make it go away. The big question is, How does one cope?

The morning my husband was diagnosed with cancer, two of these dear Louisville friends made the three-plus hour trip to Columbus. Something told them to get up before daybreak and drive to Columbus to see us. None of us knew that my husband had cancer at this point in time. It was about 8:45 and the nurse came in and said we had visitors and did I want to see them? I had no idea who had come. I walked out in the hall and there were two of my best friends with their arms open wide. Hugs and tears followed. What a blessing to see them. My husband was pleased to see them as well. In comes the doctor and asks that the room be cleared because he had to talk with the two of us. The next 30 minutes plays over and over again as my worst nightmare. The burning, screaming, stinging, deafening word "cancer." And my friends were out in the waiting room. God knew I would need them that morning. The "something" that said "Drive to Columbus" was Him, the mastermind of this 15-year-long friendship.

Those beautiful, unsuspecting, blindsided belles in Louisville have been my lifeline. God knew 15 years ago how much I would need them. One alone wouldn't be enough. God had the perfect plan for my life. Move me to Louisville, Kentucky, where waiting in the garden of life were these beautiful flowers who allow me to come to the garden and share my pain and my heartache. They listen to my words of hope; they listen as I fear for the future; they listen as I share the physical symptoms of my husband's cancer and his treatment; they listen to the hearts of my children; they listen when I can't find words; they allow me to cry. Quietly, silently they are carrying my burden with me and my family. They are strong women who believe in Jesus and encourage me when I need it most. They are my inner-circle prayer warriors. They intercede on my behalf. I can call them in the middle of the night or at the crack of dawn. They answer.

My friendship story doesn't end with the cancer diagnosis. These friends have cleaned, cooked, mulched, weeded, repaired, listened, cried, laughed, joked, invited, sorted, and lifted me and my family up to the Lord faithfully for the past seven months. Sometimes there aren't any words, and the listening is all silence. But they are always there asking, waiting, and wanting to help. These are my God friends, my sisters in Christ sent as an answer to the prayers of three faithful praying mothers. Two of the mothers have gone to be with the Lord. My mother is still praying for me today. I moved again. Tracy and I are still best friends, now just miles apart. But the Louisville gang, my functional Ya-Ya's, continue to pray for me daily, send scripture, listen and hang on to my every word, find times and places for me to escape the reality of cancer, and encourage me with words of faith and hope. They are the colorful centerpiece in

> my life. Each different, beautiful, and special, but in my life they can't stand alone. We are one in Christ. There is a song by Michael W. Smith in which he sings, "Friends are friends forever if the Lord is Lord of them." These women are my forever friends.

Don't Try This by Yourself

By now you know this, but I want to reinforce one last bit of encouragement: Don't believe you are left to yourself to tackle developing and keeping a smart mouth. The tongue is a pretty unruly creature. When I talk about this subject in seminars and retreats, I can see people sinking deeper and deeper into their seats thinking, *How am I supposed to change all of this?* James 3:8 gives insight and a great comfort about our speech: "No man can tame the tongue. It is a restless evil, full of deadly poison." While at first blush this doesn't look like good news, the statement begs the question, "Well, who can?" Thanks be to God for the loving and wise gift of the Holy Spirit who can tame anything we can't! We've turned to the book of Proverbs so many times on this topic, and our foundation comes again from Proverbs 3:5-6:

> Trust in the LORD with all your heart
> and lean not on your own understanding;
> in all your ways acknowledge him,
> and he will make your paths straight.

By the indwelling of and constant reliance on the Holy Spirit, we *can grow* into people who are loving, wise, and mature in the areas of listening, speaking, and communicating with others.

A very practical exercise we can engage in takes a page from Benjamin Franklin's history. He was renowned for his focus on positive character traits. As he was challenging himself to grow as a person, he put the virtues he thought most important on pieces of paper and concentrated on one at a time for a week. Make yourself a deck of twelve 3 x 5 cards, each with the main theme from chapters 1 through 12 (see appendix B). Start week one with the first trait. Keep the card visible where you are most likely to see it to be reminded of that week's insight. On week two, go to the next card. By the time the year is through, you will have been through your deck at least four times, and you will certainly have much wiser speech! If you live with family or have coworkers who would like to participate in this exercise with you, put a poster up of the week's trait and see what happens.

One last thought on using your smart mouth to be a good communicator and to communicate for good. Never underestimate the power of the corners of your mouth being turned upward. This nonverbal communicates volumes to the world around you. It also communicates to your brain with muscle messages that will make you actually feel better too. It is scientifically proven that smiling makes you happier just as being happy can make you smile.

God has given you the gifts necessary for being a good communicator. And you have the Spirit of God necessary to communicating for good. You have changed your world in the past with your words. You are, even today, making an impact that reaches far beyond what you can see or sense. By making great choices and relying on your potent partnership with God, you will make a difference in the lives of the people you interact with in the next 24 hours and the generations to come. Live in such a way that you can say of yourself and others will say of you, "The lips of the righteous nourish many...The tongue that brings healing is a tree of life" (Proverbs 10:21 and 15:4).

Appendix A

50 Great Questions to Ask Others

1. What are you most excited about right now?
2. What do you do for fun?
3. And then what happened?
4. What have you got to lose?
5. Where do you sense God moving in your life?
6. What are some of your important boundaries?
7. What are some of your important standards?
8. What do you do when you need to recharge your batteries?
9. What's the best thing that happened to you this week?
10. What passages of Scripture are most meaningful to you?
11. Where do you want to go on your next vacation?
12. What is your definition of success in your (spiritual, relational, financial, physical, intellectual, social) life?
13. What makes you smile?
14. How may I pray for you?
15. What are you taking away from that situation?
16. What character quality do you want to work on in yourself?

17. What are you experiencing right now?
18. What did you experience when…?
19. If you were a character in history, who would you be?
20. What does (whatever concept just said) mean to you?
21. What's your favorite artistic expression (music, painting, cartoons, poetry, fabric)?
22. If you could do it over again, what would you do?
23. What possible solutions do you see?
24. May I ask you a question?
25. May I share something with you?
26. What do you want to do for your next (birthday, anniversary, other celebration)?
27. What's your favorite way of learning something new?
28. What are you looking forward to?
29. How would you like to see this turn out?
30. What do you make of this?
31. When you're attending your eightieth birthday celebration, what do you want people to say about you?
32. What do you want? (Tone of voice is crucial.)
33. How was your week?
34. What is stopping you?
35. What are your best next steps?
36. For what are you grateful?
37. If you were going to focus on taking good care of yourself for a day, what would that look like?
38. Is there anything else? (Tone of voice is crucial.)
39. What gives you energy?

40. What have you always wanted to do but haven't?
41. What kind of support do you need?
42. What aspects of your (spiritual, financial, physical, relational, intellectual) life do you want to strengthen?
43. What are the best gifts you bring to this world?
44. What activities bring you joy, whether you're good at them or not?
45. What are your hidden talents?
46. What are five things you like about one of your favorite people?
47. Could you tell me more about...?
48. The world would be a better place if it just had more... what?
49. What do you want less of in your life right now?
50. What do you want more of in your life right now?

Appendix B

12 Key Areas of Powerful Communication

Wisdom

Honesty

Self-Care

Understanding

Clarity

Maturity

Respect

Forgiveness

Encouragement

Decency

Justice

Silence

Notes

Chapter 2—Threads of Honesty

1. William King, *Hans Christian Andersen's Fairy Tales* (Philadelphia: Running Press, 1996), p. 15.
2. Quoted in John Macionis, *Society: The Basics* (Upper Saddle River, NJ: Pearson Education, 2006), p. 97.

Chapter 3—Don't Let Your Mind Eat Junk Food

1. Catherine Marshall, *Warm Wisdom* (Nashville: J. Countryman, 2002), p. 73.

Chapter 4—Listen Up!

1. Frederick Buechner, *Listening to Your Life* (San Francisco: HarperSanFrancisco, 1992), p. 125.

Chapter 5—Straight Shooters Hit More Bull's-eyes

1. Edwin H. Friedman, *Generation to Generation: Family Process in Church and Synagogue* (New York: The Guilford Press, 1985), p. 27.

Chapter 7—Give Peace a Fighting Chance

1. Stephen R. Covey, *The Seven Habits of Highly Effective People* (New York: Simon & Schuster, 1989), p. 237.
2. Ibid., p. 239.
3. David Knox and Caroline Schacht, *Choices in Relationships,* 9th ed. (Belmont, CA: Thomson Wadsworth, 2008), p.265.
4. Ibid., p. 268.

Chapter 8—I Need to Tell You...

1. Penelope Stokes, *Simple Words of Wisdom* (Nashville: Thomas Nelson, Inc., 1998), p. 85.
2. Janet R. Pedersen, "How to Deliver Bad News in a Good Way," http://www.communicate4results.com/bad_news.htm, 2/14/2007.

Chapter 10—Threads of Forgiveness

1. Frederick Buechner, *Wishful Thinking: A Seeker's ABC* (San Francisco: HarperSanFrancisco, 1993), p. 2.
2. Quoted in Fredric and Mary Ann Brussat, *Spiritual Literacy: Reading the Sacred in Everyday Life* (New York: Scribner, 1996), p. 216.

Chapter 11—Thanks, I Needed That!

1. Les and Leslie Parrott, *Like a Kiss on the Lips* (Grand Rapids, MI: Zondervan, 1997), p. 28.

Chapter 14—The Wisdom of Silence

1. Quoted in John Shaughnessy, "SHHH!!!" *The Indianapolis Star,* Monday, April 13, 2003.
2. Frederick Buechner, *Telling Secrets: A Memoir* (New York: HarperCollins Publishers, 1991), p. 39.
3. Ibid., p. 24.

The Power of Words

1. William Barclay, *The Gospel of John,* vol. 1 (Louisville: Westminster John Knox Press, 2001), p. 32.
2. Ibid., p. 33.
3. Ibid.

Suggested Reading

Buechner, Frederick. *Telling Secrets: A Memoir.* New York: HarperCollins Publishers, 1991.

Byers, Mary M. *How to Say No and Live to Tell About It.* Eugene, OR: Harvest House Publishers, 2006.

Canfield, Jack, and Mark Victor Hansen. *The Aladdin Factor.* New York: The Berkeley Publishing Group, 1995.

Cloud, Henry, and John Townsend. *12 "Christian" Beliefs That Can Drive You Crazy.* Grand Rapids, MI: Zondervan, 1995.

Covey, Stephen R. *The 7 Habits of Highly Effective People.* New York: Simon & Schuster, 1989.

Friedman, Edwin. *Generation to Generation: Family Process in Church and Synagogue.* New York: The Guilford Press, 1985.

Good, Cynthia. *Words Every Child Must Hear.* Marietta, GA: Longstreet Press, Inc., 1994.

Gottman, John, Ph.D. *Why Marriages Succeed or Fail: And How You Can Make Yours Last.* New York: Simon & Schuster, 1994.

Hunter, James C. *The Servant: A Simple Story About the True Essence of Leadership.* New York: Crown Business, 1998.

Jeffers, Susan. *Feel the Fear...and Beyond.* New York: The Ballantine Publishing Group, 1998.

Ladd, Karol, and Terry Ann Kelly. *The Power of a Positive Friend.* West Monroe, LA: Howard Publishing Co., 2004.

Maxwell, John C., and Jim Dornan. *Becoming a Person of Influence.* Nashville: Thomas Nelson, 1997.

Pachter, Barbara. *The Power of Positive Confrontation: The Skills You Need to Know to Handle Conflicts at Work, Home, and in Life.* New York: Marlowe & Company, 2000.

Parrott, Les and Leslie. *Like a Kiss on the Lips.* Grand Rapids, MI: Zondervan, 1997.

Smedes, Lewis B. *Forgive and Forget: Healing the Hurts We Don't Deserve.* New York: Simon & Schuster, 1984.

Stone, Douglas, Bruce Patton, and Sheila Heen. *Difficult Conversations: How to Discuss What Matters Most.* New York: Penguin Putnam, Inc., 1999.

Wilkins, Richard. *When God Asks...A Chance to Change.* Nashville: Thomas Nelson Company, 2001.

Williams, Patrick, and Lloyd J. Thomas. *Total Life Coaching.* New York: Norton, 2005.

About the Author

Robin Chaddock is an insightful speaker, seminar leader, and internationally known author. She offers expert life coaching, weekly encouragement via email, and uplifting and inspirational messages for churches, civic, and corporate groups. A warm, welcoming, and wise seminar and retreat leader, she affirms the lives of her audiences and encourages change through popular topics that include "Reclaiming Your Deck Chair on the S.S. Sanity," "Top Ten Ways to Get a Smart Mouth," "Come to Your Senses," "Discovering Your Divine Assignment," and "Wise Up! Six Proverbial Keys to Light Living."

A dynamic media guest, Robin has been interviewed on national radio and television, including Cornerstone Television, Trinity Broadcasting Network, Christian Television Network, LeSea Broadcasting, Total Living Network, FamilyNet Television, Focus on the Family, and Time for Hope. She's been profiled in *The Indianapolis Star, Indianapolis Woman,* and *The Noblesville Ledger.*

Robin earned a B.A. in psychology from Indiana's Taylor University, an M.A. in theology from California's Fuller Theological Seminary, and D.Min. from Illinois' McCormick Theological Seminary. She and her husband, David, and their two children live in Indiana.

For resources to renew and refresh you, check out Robin's website:

www.RobinChaddock.com

This site is packed with uplifting, grounding, and rejuvenating materials and services that provide stress reduction, career direction, spiritual guidance, and communication tips to bring you peace and a new outlook for zesty living.

HOW TO FIND YOUR PERSONAL PATH TO SUCCESS

Keys to Living Your Purpose and Passion

ROBIN CHADDOCK

PROFESSIONAL LIFE COACH

How to Find Your Personal Path to Success

Is There More to Life?

Do you sometimes question what you're doing? Do you wonder why you're here? Robin Chaddock draws on her extensive experience as a life coach to help you find the God-given purpose that will being you joy. She takes you step-by-step through a revealing process that uncovers your primary passions and greatest strengths, and then provides a framework for discovering how to use them to achieve satisfaction and fulfillment.

You'll discover how to...

- nurture and grow your strengths
- use your talents and gifts creatively and effectively
- positively impact your sphere of influence
- bring out the best in the people around you
- develop a more intimate relationship with God

The easy-to-read chapters include fun and challenging questions to help you identify your core beliefs and clarify your goals. Knowing your personal path to success enables you to live confidently, experience happiness, encourage family and friends, and help others.